Related Family and Criminal Proceedings

Related titles by Law Society Publishing:

Child Contact
Miranda Fisher and Sarah Whitten with Noel Arnold

Child Law Handbook
Liz Goldthorpe with Pat Monro

CLSA Duty Solicitors' Handbook (3rd edn)
Andrew Keogh

Criminal Defence (3rd edn)
Roger Ede and Anthony Edwards

Prison Law (due Spring 2008)
Margaret Obi

Resolution Family Law Handbook
General Editor: Andrew Greensmith

Titles from Law Society Publishing can be ordered from all good legal bookshops or direct from our distributors, Prolog (tel. 0870 850 1422 or email **lawsociety@prolog.uk.com**). For further information or a catalogue, email our editorial and marketing office at **publishing@lawsociety.org.uk**.

Related Family and Criminal Proceedings

A Good Practice Guide

General Editor: Ananda Hall

The Law Society

First edition published 2007

ISBN 978 1 85328 609 4

Published on behalf of the Family-Criminal Interface Committee by Law Society Publishing 113 Chancery Lane, London WC2A 1PL

The Family-Criminal Interface Committee is a joint Committee established by the President of the Family Division and the Solicitor General. Copies of this Good Practice Guide are available in PDF format at:
www.family-justice-council.org.uk
and in hard copy from Prolog (tel. 0870 850 1422 or email **lawsociety@prolog.uk.com**)

Typeset by J&L Composition, Filey, North Yorkshire
Printed by Antony Rowe Ltd, Chippenham, Wilts

Contents

Foreword

Some of the most difficult cases with which the courts have to deal span both the criminal and family courts often at the same time. The children involved and their families need consistent treatment within the justice system. However, in an era of increased specialisation this can be quite difficult to achieve. Families involved in each jurisdiction are usually represented by different lawyers who know little of the other system. Yet consistency, liaison and, where possible, cooperation across the two systems are essential.

We therefore greatly welcome this initiative whose purpose is to assist criminal lawyers unfamiliar with the family justice system, and vice versa, to understand what it is their colleagues are required to do and are trying to achieve and to help them to work together in concurrent proceedings. We recognise that each system inevitably has to be run differently, and that lawyers owe different duties in each. Whilst the criminal justice system is plainly adversarial, the family system is more inquisitorial in nature. Moreover, whilst the family justice system has the welfare of the child as its paramount consideration, the criminal justice system has to accommodate concepts of public policy and the need to guarantee a fair trial to a defendant as well as recognising welfare issues.

Experience suggests that liaison between the systems, vital though it is, is more difficult to achieve than it ought to be and we hope that this guide may help to redress that. Whilst it is written by practising lawyers principally for their legal colleagues, we believe that it may also be of use to others – police, social workers and guardians – who play indispensable roles in the administration of justice.

We pay tribute to the team who have put this guide together – those who work in this area will be very much in their debt. We are pleased too that the Law Society has agreed to publish it. We commend this guide to all who work with cases involving children and their families and who wish to see closer cooperation between us and better outcomes for children.

Sir Igor Judge
President of the Queen's Bench Division

Sir Mark Potter
President of the Family Division

Vera Baird, QC, MP
Solicitor General

Acknowledgements

This guide has been drafted by experienced legal professionals in private practice and at the Bar, the CPS and local government. It has been produced at the request of the Family-Criminal Interface Committee, which is a Committee jointly established by the President of the Family Division and the Solicitor General, and chaired by the Hon Mr Justice Hedley, High Court Family Division. The Committee includes representatives of the family and criminal judiciaries, Justices' Clerks Association, Magistrates' Association, Family and Criminal Procedure Rules Committees, Criminal Prosecution Service, Association of Chief Police Officers, Child and Family Court Advisory and Support Service, Association of Directors of Social Services, National Probation Directorate, Ministry of Justice, Department for Children Schools and Families, and the Home Office.

The Committee is grateful for the assistance of the drafting group:

- Ananda Hall, Solicitor (General Editor)
- Nadine Tilbury, Crown Prosecution Service
- Judith Rowe QC, Family Law Bar Association
- Sam Whittam, Family Law Bar Association
- John Riley, Criminal Law Bar Association
- Nabila Zulfiqar, Birmingham City Council Legal Services
- Barbara Corbett, Law Society (Family Law Committee)
- Angus McBride, Law Society (Crime Committee)

List of abbreviations

ABE	Achieving Best Evidence
ACPO	Association of Chief Police Officers
ADSS	Association of Directors of Social Services*
CAAC	Children Act Advisory Committee
Cafcass	Children and Family Court Advisory and Support Service
CPIA 1996	Criminal Procedure and Investigations Act 1996
CPS	Crown Prosecution Service
ECHR	European Convention on Human Rights
EPO	emergency protection order
FCIC	Family-Criminal Interface Committee
FHDRA	first hearing dispute resolution appointment
FPC	Family Proceedings Court
FPR 1991	Family Proceedings Rules 1991, SI 1991/1247
IDVC	Integrated Domestic Violence Court
LA	local authority
NSPCC	National Society for the Prevention of Cruelty to Children
PCMH	plea and case management hearing
PHA 1997	Protection from Harassment Act 1997
PHA order	Protection from Harassment Act 1997 order
PII	public interest immunity
SDVC	Specialist Domestic Violence Court
YJCEA 1999	Youth Justice and Criminal Evidence Act 1999

* The ADSS no longer exists and has been replaced by the Association of Directors of Children's Services.

Glossary

ABE interview An interview of a child following the guidance 'Achieving Best Evidence in Criminal Proceedings'. Also known as a 'memorandum' interview.

Advance information A summary of the prosecution allegations provided at the first hearing.

Care order An order placing a child in the care of the designated local authority. This order confers on the local authority parental responsibility for the child.

Defence case statement This statement will set out in general terms the nature of the defence and the issues which are contested in criminal proceedings. Details must be given of any alibis. There is no duty on the defence to serve such a statement in the magistrates' court although it is sometimes served in order to trigger further disclosure of unused material.

Emergency Protection Order An order authorising the urgent removal of a child into the care of the designated local authority, or to prevent the child's removal from the place in which the child was accommodated immediately prior to the making of the order. This order confers on the local authority parental responsibility for the child.

Family proceedings In this guide, 'family proceedings' includes both Children Act 1989 proceedings and Family Law Act 1996 (domestic violence) proceedings.

Family proceedings court Magistrates' court with jurisdiction to hear family proceedings.

Final directions hearing *See* Pre-hearing review.

Form 78 If the police are called to an incident in which a child is involved, they have a duty to inform the local authority using this form.

Either way offences An offence which can be tried in either the magistrates' or Crown Court.

Indictable only offences An offence which must be tried in the Crown Court.

Initial disclosure Statements, copies of exhibits and a schedule of 'unused material' in criminal proceedings. The prosecution are required to serve this on the defence prior to trial.

Intimidated witnesses Defined in Youth Justice and Criminal Evidence Act 1999, s.17 to include those whose quality of evidence is likely to be diminished by reason of fear or distress in connection with testifying in the proceedings, taking into account the nature and alleged circumstances of the offence or their personal circumstances and any behaviour towards them of the accused or associated persons.

Memorandum interview *See* ABE interview.

Non-molestation order An order which usually prohibits the respondent from using or threatening violence against the applicant and any named children, or from harassing or molesting the applicant, or encouraging any other person to do so. A non-molestation order may include a prohibition against the respondent coming within a specified distance of the applicant's home, the applicant and named children personally, and other specified locations. *See also* Part IV proceedings.

Occupation order An order regulating the entitlement of parties to occupy a dwelling.

Part IV proceedings Proceedings under Family Law Act 1996, Part IV. These are private law proceedings brought between individuals in cases where violence or harassment, actual or threatened, arises between persons in familial-type relationships. Applicants may seek a non-molestation order (injuncting the respondent from using or threatening violence or harassment against the applicant) and/or an occupation order (which determines each party's rights to occupy the family home).

PHA order An order under the Protection from Harassment Act 1997 restraining a person from harassing another.

Pre-hearing review A hearing taking place shortly before the final hearing in family proceedings to confirm that all necessary evidence has been collected and that the proceedings are ready for final determination. Also known as a final directions hearing.

Professional acting in furtherance of the protection of children This is defined in Family Proceedings Rules 1991, SI 1991/1247, rule 10.20A(5) to include for the purposes of those Rules:

(a) an officer of a local authority exercising child protection functions,

(b) a police officer who is –
  (i) exercising powers under s46 of the Children Act 1989, or
  (ii) serving in a child protection unit or paedophile unit of a police force

(c) any professional attending a child protection conference or review in relation to a child who is the subject of the proceedings to which the information relates, or

(d) an officer of the NSPCC.

Public interest immunity This doctrine prevents material from being disclosed and adduced in the usual way whenever it is held that the public interest in non-disclosure outweighs the public interest that, for the proper administration of justice, the court should have the fullest possible access to all relevant material and that the accused person should have a fair trial. The prosecution must make application to the court in relation to any such material. Information can never be withheld from the defence if it would cause injustice or affect the fairness of the proceedings.

Public law outline A case management protocol which from April 2008 will govern the conduct of care proceedings, with an emphasis on pre-proceedings preparation by the local authority.

'Re L' hearing A fact-finding hearing held in family proceedings in accordance with the guidance of the Court of Appeal in *Re L, M, V and H* [2000] 2 FLR 334, so that the court can make findings as to disputed allegations of domestic violence, which one party is relying on to prevent contact between a child and an alleged perpetrator.

Section 7 report A welfare report prepared pursuant to Children Act 1989, s.7 by an officer of Cafcass or the local authority, in private law children proceedings at the court's direction, on matters relating to the child's welfare.

Section 16 witnesses Witnesses in criminal proceedings who are children and vulnerable adults, under Youth Justice and Criminal Evidence Act 1999, s.16. *See* Vulnerable witnesses.

Section 17 witnesses Witnesses in criminal proceedings who suffer intimidation/fear or distress, under Youth Justice and Criminal Evidence Act 1999, s.17. *See* Intimidated witnesses.

Section 37 report A report prepared pursuant to Children Act 1989, s.37 by the appropriate local authority, at the direction of the court in any family proceedings in which a question arises with respect to the welfare of the child, it appearing to the court that it may be appropriate for a care or supervision order to be made.

Section 38(6) assessment An assessment authorised under Children Act 1989, s.38(6) to assess in detail the parents' relationship with and ability to parent the child, in either a residential unit or the community.

Section 47 enquiries An enquiry commenced by a local authority in accordance with its duty under Children Act 1989, s.47 to investigate a child's circumstances and safeguard the child's welfare in any case where there is reasonable cause to suspect that the child is suffering, or likely to suffer, significant harm.

Section 51 sendings In criminal proceedings, Crime and Disorder Act 1998, s.51 abolished committal proceedings for indictable only offences and created a new system of 'sending' such offences (together with related either way or summary only offences) to the Crown Court for trial.

Section 53 transfers In criminal proceedings, Criminal Justice Act 1991, s.53 provides for a transfer procedure from the magistrates' court to the Crown Court for certain cases involving children as victims or witnesses of certain sexual offences or offences of violence.

Special measures These are available for vulnerable and intimidated witnesses and some defendants in criminal proceedings under Part II of the Youth Justice and Criminal Evidence Act 1999. They provide the court with options for the way a witness gives evidence. For example, by live TV link or from behind screens.

Specialist Domestic Violence Courts Magistrates' courts which operate a clustering system for criminal cases involving domestic violence. Support and advocacy services are made available to victims, including help at court, and advice on housing, benefits and safety.

Summary only offences Offences that can usually only be tried in the magistrates' court.

Supervision order An order appointing the designated local authority to advise, assist and befriend the supervised child, to take such steps as are necessary to give effect to the order, and to consider whether to apply to the court if the order is not wholly complied with.

Vulnerable witnesses Defined in Youth Justice and Criminal Evidence Act 1999, s.16 to include all children aged under 17 years (in relation to all offences), and adults who suffer from mental disorder; have a significant impairment of intelligence and social functioning; or have a physical disability or disorder (in relation to all offences).

CHAPTER 1

Overview

1.1 INTRODUCTION

Some of the most difficult of matters involve concurrent, or imminent, criminal and family proceedings. A family who has experienced the suspicious death, injury or other abuse of a child may be not only the subject of criminal proceedings, but also subject to the involvement of the local authority (LA) and often the commencement of care proceedings in respect of any other remaining children. Equally, families who have experienced domestic violence are likely to be involved not only in criminal proceedings, but also in private law proceedings regarding contact and residence issues in respect of the children.

It can be challenging to cross smoothly the boundaries between family and criminal jurisdictions. The prevailing ethos in the respective jurisdictions and the professional duties upon lawyers differ widely consequent upon the differing expectations of the court in each jurisdiction. Family proceedings are, fundamentally, conducted upon the principles of openness and full disclosure, with fewer restrictions on the admissibility of evidence. Criminal proceedings are governed by very different expectations. Further, whilst criminal proceedings are held in public, family proceedings – and the documents filed in them – are confidential. Numerous agencies and professionals can become involved with families, each having differing responsibilities, occasionally leading to 'silo working' where professionals are effectively cut off from each other, rather than mutual cooperation.

This guide aims to provide:

(a)   a general overview of the jurisdictions involved;

(b)   clarification of the duties, obligations and responsibilities of the various statutory agencies, but mainly the police and social services;

(c)   a reminder of the need to ensure early communication between the parties and judges;

(d)   reference to practice directions and protocols which are already being used around the country; and

(e)   assistance in enabling the criminal and civil processes to be concluded as swiftly as possible with all relevant information.

1.2 FAMILY PROCEEDINGS

In this guide, 'family proceedings' includes both Children Act 1989 proceedings and Family Law Act 1996 (domestic violence) proceedings.

Applications under the Children Act 1989 can be made privately by individuals, or by public local authorities, and in some cases the NSPCC. In every case concerning the upbringing of a child, the judge or magistrates hearing the application will have two thoughts uppermost in mind: first, that the welfare of the child is of paramount importance and the first consideration of the court; and second, that any delay is likely to prejudice the welfare of the child.

Unnecessary delay is specifically proscribed by the Children Act 1989. In public law care proceedings there is a national Judicial Case Management Protocol[1] which provides for applications to be disposed of within a 40-week time period. This includes assessment work, information gathering and the making of final proposals and plans by all parties for consideration by the court.

There is an ethos of full and frank disclosure of information between the parties in Children Act 1989 proceedings. Parties are obliged to provide the court with all relevant information which may impact on the court's determination relating to the upbringing of the child, regardless of whether or not it is harmful to that party's case. Hearsay evidence

---

[1]   The protocol will be replaced by the Public Law Outline by April 2008. The 40-week deadline will not change, although it is expected that cases will be resolved more quickly where possible.

may be admitted. The court makes its findings or decision on a balance of probabilities.

1.3 CRIMINAL PROCEEDINGS

The criminal justice system aims to punish crime, protect the public and rehabilitate offenders. In addition to preventing crime, the police have a duty to investigate crime, secure evidence and apprehend offenders. The Crown Prosecution Service (CPS) has a duty to prosecute offenders if there is sufficient evidence and it is in the public interest. At trial, some hearsay evidence is admissible and each element of any offence must be established beyond reasonable doubt. The Probation Service has a duty to report to the court on bail and sentencing, and to monitor the compliance of released offenders with licence conditions.

The criminal courts have recently adopted case management practices, which are now integral to criminal procedure. There is now greater emphasis on pre-trial disclosure of evidence, supported by comprehensive Criminal Procedure Rules. In some types of proceedings (such as persistent young offenders), there are time limits on the conclusion of proceedings.

1.4 APPLICABILITY OF THE HUMAN RIGHTS ACT 1998

The Human Rights Act 1998 came into force on 2 October 2000 and incorporates into UK law certain provisions of the European Convention on Human Rights. Within both jurisdictions, the European Convention on Human Rights gives every person:

(a) *The right to respect for private and family life, home and correspondence (Art.8).* This is a qualified right which may be interfered with where it is in the interests of national security, public safety or the economic well being of the country, for the prevention of disorder or crime, for the protection of health or morals, or for the protection of the rights and freedoms of others.

(b) *The right to a fair trial (Art.6).* This is a special right which means that it cannot be balanced against other public interests. Every person is entitled to a fair and public hearing within a reasonable time by an independent and impartial tribunal established by law.

1.5 INTERFACE BETWEEN THE FAMILY AND CRIMINAL JURISDICTIONS

Within both jurisdictions, allegations may be made of physical harm, emotional harm, sexual abuse, neglect or domestic violence (including psychological harm).

Potential complaints or referrals may be received from a range of sources, including:

- children;
- parents;
- other family members;
- carers and child minders;
- teachers;
- probation officers;
- voluntary agencies and family centres;
- midwives and health visitors;
- doctors and nurses;
- police;
- social workers and mental health workers;
- Cafcass officers; and
- foster carers.

Police and local authorities will most likely be the first agencies to become involved with individuals, children or families where such allegations are made. If the police are called to an incident in which a child is involved, they have a duty to inform the LA using a form 78. Conversely, if the LA receives a referral which involves the commission of a crime, they are obliged to inform the police, following the guidelines in *Working Together 2006*.[2]

Where police and the LA are involved together regarding a referral, there follows a process of both *joint* and *individual* investigation by each statutory agency. A joint strategy meeting or meetings will be held by the key officers from each agency to ensure that joint working is effectively achieved and a joint strategy devised. A divergence occurs

---

[2] Available online (**www.everychildmatters.gov.uk/resources-and-practice/IG00060/**).

following the initial investigation stage, whereupon police will pursue alleged perpetrators and the LA will act to protect children at risk of harm.

Evidence in the form of statements and reports is provided to the court in Children Act proceedings to establish risk, or likelihood of risk, of significant harm on a balance of probabilities. Where LAs initiate care proceedings, there is a duty to promote reasonable contact, which may be supervised and in a neutral setting, between children and parents.

The police obtain witness statements and undertake recorded interviews (sometimes video recorded) with alleged perpetrators, with a view to building a case to establish a realistic prospect of conviction. Child witnesses/complainants may be interviewed on video (called an 'Achieving Best Evidence' (ABE) interview).

Problems tend to arise where:

(a)   parties to either set of proceedings request access to evidence gathered to date by the other;

(b)   the status of the police investigation (e.g. when it will be concluded) is unknown or delayed;

(c)   access to information or evidence is denied or delayed;

(d)   bail conditions imposed on those charged directly affect the children (e.g. contact with parents);

(e)   children may continue to make disclosures, for example of sexual abuse, when placed in a 'safe environment' such as a foster home;

(f)   therapy for children is unnecessarily delayed pending the criminal trial;

(g)   the criminal trial is listed to take place after the 40-week period within which care proceedings need to be concluded. If parents are alleged perpetrators of abuse, this will impact directly on the long-term plans for the children as well as any contact;

(h)   a finding of fact needs to be made in the care proceedings in order to establish whether the threshold criteria under Children Act 1989, s.31 has been met, and state intervention into family life is justified. Such a finding may be made by a Family Proceedings Court, county court or the High Court. Whilst such a finding may not be admissible in the criminal proceedings (depending on the circumstances), it may be highly relevant to decisions relating to bail and whether or not to prosecute;

(i)   defendants' solicitors or the police make requests for access to
        LA files which then require a public interest immunity (PII)
        hearing.

The ethos of encouraging openness and frankness in family proceedings
ought not to be lost. However, we know that defendants can benefit
from the gap between the two jurisdictions, admitting matters in a
family court to enhance the chance of eventual reunion with a child,
then denying matters in a criminal court. The result of this is that the
victim is either required to give evidence, or is led to retract her
evidence, whilst the defendant is able to rely on the knowledge that no
reference can be made to any matters dealt with in the family court.

1.6   ABOUT THIS GUIDE

This guide is intended to assist practitioners and the court in dealing
with such issues. **Chapter 2** begins with 'route maps' to each of the relevant jurisdictions, including an overview of the hearings one can expect
to take place, and the documents and other evidence one can expect to
be created in the proceedings. **Chapter 3** goes on to address the general
principles surrounding disclosure of information as well as documents
and other evidence, and identifies the different approaches adopted in
the respective family and criminal fields. **Chapter 4** explains the way in
which joint case management hearings can be utilised effectively to deal
with concurrent proceedings. **Chapters 5** and **6** explore the specific
issues which arise in relation to pre-trial therapy and pre-trial contact.
Chapter 7 explains the effect of s.98(2) of the Children Act 1989,
Chapter 8 deals with public interest immunity and **Chapter 9** explores
the use of special measures. The guide then concludes with some practical examples in **Chapter 10**, followed by a collection of appendices
providing useful protocol forms and contacts.

Whilst intended to provide valuable practical assistance and information, this guide also has a higher aim. There has been an apparent gulf
between those practising in the criminal and family fields, and a genuine
lack of mutual understanding, which can lead to serious failings when
neither the parties nor the court is provided with all the relevant
information. When documents fail to arrive, or information is not
shared as it should be, the court proceeds without complete information
and poor outcomes can result. It is hoped that this guide will increase

understanding and dialogue, and assist all practitioners to close the jurisdictional gap.

This guide comes with one 'health warning': we operate in an era of persistent change. Whilst the information contained in this guide is correct at the time of writing, practitioners are advised to be aware that changes may subsequently have taken place. In addition, whilst providing an overview as to best practice, this guide does not include details of local practices and protocols that may have been adopted and be working successfully. It is always advisable to investigate what local arrangements exist.

CHAPTER 2

Route maps

This chapter is divided into the following sections:

- criminal proceedings route map;
- care proceedings route map;
- private law Children Act 1989 proceedings route map;
- Family Law Act 1996 (Part IV) (non-molestation/occupation orders) proceedings route map.

Each route map outlines the general steps of the relevant proceedings, along with documents that are to be produced at each stage.

2.1   CRIMINAL PROCEEDINGS ROUTE MAP

Step	Documents produced
The investigation The suspect may be arrested or attend an interview as a volunteer. An arrest can take place if there is reasonable suspicion that the suspect has committed an offence and the arrest is necessary. A police interview will be conducted under caution, with the suspect advised of the right to independent and free legal advice. The meaning of 'the caution' will be explained. A legal representative should, unless the suspect elects otherwise, be present to advise on the consequence of any answer that the suspect may give during the course of police questioning and of the right to maintain silence. The suspect will also be advised of the consequence of remaining silent should the matter proceed to court. In brief, the suspect has the right to silence but if a fact is not mentioned in interview at the police station whilst under caution which is later relied on in court in the suspect's defence, the jury or	• *Transcript of police interview* • *Witness statements* • *Custody records* • *Documents relating to samples taken from a suspect (DNA, fingerprints, etc.)* • *Police notes taken during witness interviews*

Step	Documents produced
magistrates can draw a proper inference from the failure to mention the fact at the earliest opportunity.	• *Forensic evidence*
Witness interviews will also be conducted by the police. Vulnerable witnesses will be interviewed in accordance with police procedure, usually on videotape.	• *Expert reports* • *Antecedent history of defendants and witnesses*

Custody

If the suspect is in custody, there are time limits dictating the length of detention. Before the conclusion of the relevant time limit, the police, advised by the Crown Prosecution Service (CPS), must decide whether the suspect is to be released on 'police bail' which requires the suspect to return to a named police station on a specified date/time, whether they are to be charged with an offence, or whether no further action is to be taken. The prosecution can also decide to divert a suspect from the criminal justice process by means of cautioning.

In cases where there are mental health issues then the Mental Health Act 1983 may be invoked.

Bail

Where the suspect is released on 'police bail' in order for the CPS to make a decision on prosecution then conditions can be imposed on the police bail. It is only in these circumstances that conditions can be imposed on bail prior to charge. Once a suspect is charged with an offence then bail conditions can be imposed, which may include conditions prohibiting contact with specified persons or going to geographical areas.

• Police bail form

Charge

In most cases, the decision on charge is made by the CPS. The decision is taken in accordance with the Code for Crown Prosecutors. The prosecutor must be satisfied that there is a realistic prospect of a conviction (having reviewed all the evidence available) and that it is in the public interest to prosecute.

• Charge sheet

Bail/remand

Upon charge, the defendant can be granted bail by the police to attend at the nearest magistrates' court. The police can impose conditions on bail.

• Police bail form

If bail is refused by the police (for example, on grounds of fear of interference with the course of justice, fear that the defendant will fail to surrender or fear of further

Step	Documents produced

offences) then the accused must be brought before the
next available magistrates' court who will then hear from
the prosecution and defence on whether bail should be
granted. There is a presumption of bail in favour of the
defendant and the defence will invariably offer various
conditions in order to satisfy any concerns.

- *Record of court*
  bail conditions
  (on court file,
  and by CPS)[2]

If bail is not granted, the defendant will be remanded in
custody. The defendant can make a further application at
the next magistrates' court appearance, or appeal a
refusal of bail to a Crown Court judge.

If bail is granted, the CPS can, in certain circumstances,
appeal to a Crown Court judge.

If conditional bail is granted and a complaint is made
that the defendant has breached the bail conditions, the
defendant will be apprehended and returned to court for
review of his or her bail.

In many areas Specialist Domestic Violence Court[1] (SDVC)
systems have been implemented. These are magistrates'
courts which operate a clustering or 'fast-track' list on
specified days of the week dealing particularly with
domestic violence cases. Support and independent
advocacy services are made available to victims at court,
and general advice on issues including housing, benefits
and safety is available.

Classification of offences

'Summary only offences' are tried and sentenced at the
magistrates' court. There is a right of appeal against
conviction and sentence to the Crown Court.

'Either way' offences can be tried in either the Crown
Court or the magistrates' court. If the defendant pleads
guilty, the magistrates' court can commit to the Crown
Court for sentence if its sentencing powers are insuffi-
cient. If the defendant pleads not guilty, or no plea is
indicated, the magistrates' court will decide jurisdiction.
If it accepts jurisdiction, then the defendant can either
consent to be tried in the magistrates' court or can elect
to be tried in the Crown Court.

---

[1] SDVC resource manual (**www.crimereduction.gov.uk/domesticviolence/domesticviolence59.htm**).
[2] In domestic violence cases, the police/CPS will ensure that the complainant has been informed
    about the bail position before the defendant leaves court (see 10.3, question 8). Complainants
    should be given clear information by the CPS/police as to the procedure to be followed if bail
    conditions are breached.

Step	Documents produced

'Indictable only' offences must be heard in the Crown Court.

Youth offenders

Any person between the ages of 10 and 17 inclusive will usually be tried before the Youth Court unless an exception applies. The four exceptions which either permit or require the magistrates to send or commit the defendant for trial in the Crown Court are where the young person is:

(a) charged with an indictable offence jointly with an adult who is sent for trial;

(b) charged with murder;

(c) jointly charged with an adult and the court considers it necessary in the interests of justice to commit them both for trial;

(d) charged with an offence mentioned in the Powers of the Criminal Courts (Sentencing) Act 2000, s.91, and the court considers that the sentencing court should have available to it the possibility of sentencing the offender to be detained at Her Majesty's pleasure.

Procedure

The procedure depends on the classification of the offence.

Proceedings for 'either way' offences commence before the magistrates' court where plea before venue and mode of trial proceedings will take place. If it is decided that the case is to be heard in the Crown Court or if the defendant has elected Crown Court trial, the case will be adjourned for committal proceedings. The material making up the evidence (including witness statements, etc.) will be served on the defence and committal proceedings will take place thereafter at the magistrates' court which will then formally commit the case for trial to the Crown Court.

In proceedings for 'indictable only' offences, the first hearing will take place before the magistrates' court where a section 51 transfer will take place. The case will be immediately sent to the Crown Court where it may be listed for a preliminary hearing, or a plea and case management hearing (PCMH) (at which the judge will direct timescales for the service of prosecution material and any 'unused' material) (see below).

Step	Documents produced

Thereafter the defendants charged with 'either way' or 'indictable only' offences will appear before a judge for a PCMH. This is the stage at which the defendant will plead guilty or not guilty. In the event of a not guilty plea, further directions will be made by the judge in order to prepare the matter for trial. At this hearing the prosecution should be in possession of convenient and inconvenient dates for any witnesses.

Evidence

In 'either way' cases, the defence is entitled to 'advance information', which is a summary of the prosecution allegations and is provided at the first hearing. For committal hearings, the prosecution will provide committal papers.

Prior to trial in either court, the prosecution is required to serve statements, copies of exhibits and a schedule of 'unused material' (all of this together is called 'initial disclosure'). The schedule of unused material is other material which has been obtained by the police during the course of the investigation which does not form part of the evidence against the defendant. The prosecution must review all of this material and serve any material on the defence which might reasonably be said to undermine the prosecution or assist the defence.

The disclosure of evidence and unused material is dealt with under the Criminal Procedure and Investigations Act 1996.

In any cases tried in the Crown Court the defence has a duty to serve a 'defence case statement' on the prosecution. This statement will set out in general terms the nature of the accused's defence and the issues which are contested. Details must be given of any alibis. There is no duty on the defence to serve such a statement in the magistrates' court, although it is sometimes served in order to trigger further disclosure of unused material.

The CPS must review its unused material in the light of the defence case statement and decide whether there is any other material which might reasonably be said to undermine the prosecution and/or assist the defence in the light of the defence set out within the defence case statement. This duty is an ongoing duty of review.

The CPS must decide whether any disclosure is so sensitive that it should not be disclosed to the defence and an application be made for that material to be covered by

- *Advance information*
- *Committal papers*
- *Schedule of undisclosed material*
- *Statements and copies of exhibits*
- *Defence case statement*

13

Step	Documents produced

public interest immunity (PII). The prosecution must make application to the court in relation to any such material.

The doctrine of PII prevents material from being disclosed and adduced in the usual way whenever it is held that the public interest in non-disclosure outweighs the public interest that, for the proper administration of justice, the court should have the fullest possible access to all relevant material and that the accused person should have a fair trial. Information can never be withheld from the defence if it would cause injustice or affect the fairness of the proceedings.

Expert evidence

During the proceedings evidence will be adduced by both the prosecution and defence, which may include experts' reports. There is a duty on the defence to serve on the prosecution, prior to trial, any expert evidence upon which they intend to rely.

In contrast to family proceedings, there is little oversight by the court of the obtaining of expert evidence. During the criminal investigation, the police will wish to keep developments confidential until they have interviewed the suspect. There will be little or no input from the accused's legal team, and there is limited court control over the selection and instruction of the prosecution's experts.

Equally, there is little court control over the selection and instruction of experts by the defence. In the event that the defence obtains an expert report which is unhelpful to its case, it is under no obligation to disclose it to the court or the prosecution. Part 24 of the Criminal Procedure Rules 2005, SI 2005/384 imposes a duty on the parties to disclose any expert evidence that they intend to introduce.

The collation of prosecution evidence, including obtaining evidence from third parties

The Criminal Procedure and Investigations Act 1996 requires the prosecution to provide disclosure of information in its possession where that material might reasonably be expected to assist the defendant's defence or undermine the prosecution. Where the CPS is a member of a multi-agency Local Safeguarding Children Board (previously called Area Child Protection Committees), documentation produced by the Board shall be considered to be within the possession of the CPS.

Step	Documents produced

This includes documentation regarding child death reviews, statutory domestic homicide reviews and such like.

The prosecution may also be aware of relevant information or documentation which is held by third parties, and therefore is not yet in its actual possession. Third parties holding such information will often include local authorities, health agencies, education authorities and Cafcass. If the third party information is held by the local authority (LA), the CPS should make use of the national ADSS/CPS/ACPO Protocol on obtaining information from LAs (providing that it has been locally implemented). If the material has already been filed in family court proceedings, there must be compliance with the Family Proceedings Rules 1991 (see Chapter 3, section 3.3, below). Once the prosecution is aware of the existence of relevant material, it has a duty to request disclosure from the third party.

If the defence asks the prosecution whether it intends to seek disclosure of particular information and the prosecution indicates that it does not, then the defence should approach the third party and request the information. If the agency declines the request, the defence may apply for a witness summons against the relevant authority. The summons will require the agency's attendance at court with its documentation, to enable argument before a judge who will review the documentation for relevance against a set of criteria.

It can often be difficult to obtain information held by third parties. It is not uncommon for agencies to seek to protect their records, and to be concerned about issues of confidentiality. It is, however, important that all parties work together to ensure that eleventh-hour discoveries of crucial information are avoided. Parties should give early consideration to the third parties likely to hold relevant documentation, and engage in early discussion about the sharing of that information. In some regions, the high quality of the relationship and communication between the court, the CPS, defence and LAs enables information sharing issues to be dealt with efficiently.

Disclosure hearings

The defence may apply to the court under Criminal Procedure and Investigations Act 1996, s.8 where it believes that the prosecution holds material which might reasonably be expected to assist the defendant's defence or undermine the prosecution and which has not been disclosed to the defence.

- *Witness summons*

Step	Documents produced
The defence may also request the court to issue a third party witness summons in order to require an agency to bring to court relevant documentation.	

Trial

At trial 'special measures' may be applied for by either the prosecution or defence if the case involves a vulnerable or intimidated witness. If special measures are granted, the court may allow evidence by video link or allow other measures (such as screening of witnesses) (see Chapter 9). Defendants can give evidence by live link in exceptional cases.

Sentencing and orders

Step	Documents produced
At the conclusion of the trial, a finding of guilty or not guilty will be made. The burden of proof is on the prosecution to prove the case to the required standard of proof which is 'beyond reasonable doubt'.	• *Record of verdict* • *Pre-sentence report*
If the defendant is found guilty, the court may order reports including a pre-sentence report (to be prepared by the Probation Service), psychiatric report and/or medical report. If a defendant is found guilty his or her bail position will be reviewed.	• *Psychiatric report* • *Medical report* • *Record of sentence (taken by CPS)*
Sentences may include custodial sentences, a wide variety of community-based penalties and/or orders (e.g. compensation, restraining or anti-social behaviour orders).	
The court also has the power, on entering a finding of not guilty, nevertheless to make a restraining order under Protection from Harassment Act 1997, s.5A (as amended by Domestic Violence, Crime and Victims Act 2004, s.12, not yet in force) if the court considers it necessary to do so to protect the person from harassment by the defendant. Breach of a restraining order is a criminal offence.	• *Protection from Harassment Act (PHA) order*

2.2   CARE PROCEEDINGS ROUTE MAP

A 'blueprint' for the progress and management of every set of care proceedings was originally set out in the Protocol for Judicial Case Management in Public Law Children Act Cases, which set out a route map of steps to the conclusion of the case. Those steps are to be revised by the Public Law Outline after April 2008. The overall aim, however, will not change.

The overall aim in care proceedings is that the final hearing should be concluded by the 40th week from the issue of proceedings, and earlier if possible. Section 1(2) of the Children Act 1989 states that delay in disposing of proceedings and deciding a child's long-term placement will normally be contrary to the best interests of the child. The family court will usually not, therefore, delay a fact-finding or final hearing of care proceedings to await the outcome of criminal proceedings, unless some detriment would be caused to the children if the care proceedings were not adjourned.[3]

The Protocol, and in its place the Public Law Outline, identify the key issues to be considered at each of these hearings. One key issue in concurrent family and criminal cases tends to be the issue of disclosure of documents and information from one jurisdiction into the other. Such disclosure issues will be considered by the family court early in the proceedings, and will be kept under review by the court at subsequent directions hearings.

The issue of disclosure can also arise at the final hearing – most commonly in relation to the findings made by the family court judge about allegations which may also be under police investigation, or may be the subject of a concurrent prosecution.

Step	Documents produced
Referral	
Referral received by the LA.	*A copy of the referral form will be kept on the LA file*
LA investigation	
Allegations of a child being harmed, or being at risk of significant harm, may arise in various situations. The main circumstances in which they lead eventually to care proceedings are as follows:	*LA may prepare:* • *a Core Assessment*
(a) *The allegations may arise within an ongoing investigation* – for instance, where issues of general neglect have already alerted the LA and led to the involvement of the LA.	• *Child Protection Conference reports and minutes*
(b) *The allegations may arise without any history at all* – for instance, where a parent complains to the authorities; where a teacher, a doctor or other third party reports concerns based on their professional	

[3] *Re TB (Care Proceedings: Criminal Trial)* [1995] 2 FLR 801.

17

Step	Documents produced

observations; or where such professionals report an allegation made to them by the child.

(c) *The allegations may first come to the attention of the police who then report them on to the LA.*

(d) *The allegations may arise within a court-directed investigation within private law proceedings where the court itself takes the view that the LA may need to become involved.* In these circumstances the court may direct the appropriate authority to undertake a 'section 37 investigation' of the child's circumstances.[4]

(e) *Allegations may come to light during enquiries undertaken by Cafcass in private law proceedings.*

The LA is under a duty to investigate all child protection allegations it receives. Section 47(1) of the Children Act 1989 says:

Where a local authority –

(a) are informed that a child who lives, or is found, in their area –

(ii) is in police protection; or

. . .

(b) have reasonable cause to suspect that a child who lives, or is found, in their area is suffering, or is likely to suffer, significant harm

the authority shall make, or cause to be made, such enquiries as they consider necessary to enable them to decide whether they should take any action to safeguard or promote the child's welfare.

All agencies, including the LA, are under a duty to work together when carrying out an investigation (including education, health authorities and the police): *Working Together to Safeguard Children* (2006).

Where the allegation relates to a criminal offence, there will be joint police and LA components to the investigation. Any interview of the child will be carried out jointly by police and the LA following the guidance 'Achieving Best Evidence in Criminal Proceedings' (often called an 'ABE' or 'memorandum' interview). Despite the many differences between care and criminal proceedings, it is vital in each that the evidence of children is obtained properly and reliably.

---

[4] In domestic violence cases, the CPS will try to ensure that the complainant has been informed about the bail position before the defendant leaves court.

Step	Documents produced

There will, however, be separate elements to the investigation, because:

(a)   there are different aims in the separate proceedings – care proceedings are concerned with the welfare of the child, whereas criminal proceedings are concerned with establishing the guilt of the suspect;

(b)   there are different rules of evidence – far more evidence is admissible in civil than criminal proceeding, both lay and expert;

(c)   there are different standards of proof in the two proceedings.

In most cases, however, the results of each separate element of the investigation are likely to be extremely important to the other. To take an obvious example, in a case of non-accidental injury to a child, both the police and the LA will need to gather the evidence of the relevant treating doctors to establish the relevant facts. Thereafter, the two agencies may approach different experts to advise on the findings of the treating team. Each agency will be interested in the views of the experts instructed by the other.

Whereas the child may be interviewed by police with the LA present, the LA has no role in the police interview of the parents or other adult suspects. It does have a keen interest in seeing what the parents or adult suspects have said, of course, but may often face a frustrating wait before it is able to find out. Despite a wish to cooperate, the police may well be operating under very different constraints to those of the LA – for instance, they may require their investigations to remain confidential until more issues have been put to the accused in interviews, which may not be scheduled to take place for weeks or even months, whilst the LA really needs to know what the accused are saying in respect of the allegations against them. If the accused are the parents, they may well be refusing to disclose their position to the LA precisely because of their fear of the consequences within the criminal investigation.

If there is an allegation made against a professional, then there may also be disciplinary procedures taking place in which information is shared.

Step	Documents produced

Police protection

If necessary, the police may take the child into temporary police protection for up to 72 hours.

A police officer may remove a child into suitable accommodation, or take steps to ensure that a child is not removed from a place (for example, a hospital) if the officer has reasonable cause to believe that the child would otherwise be likely to suffer significant harm. A child can be kept under police protection for a maximum of 72 hours. No court order is required.

• *Police form*

Issue of care proceedings (for either emergency protection order or care order)

The first application to court will be either for an emergency protection order (EPO) or for a care order. In each case the LA will take the decision whether to issue proceedings entirely independently of the decision of the prosecuting authorities about whether to prosecute. In many cases of alleged child abuse, there may never be sufficient evidence for a criminal prosecution.

• *C1 and C11 application forms*
• *Social work chronology*
• *Social work statement*
• *Interim care plan*

The timing of the two decisions will almost certainly be entirely different. Criminal proceedings can only begin once the investigation is largely complete, however long that process may take. By contrast, an LA must take urgent action to protect a child as soon as there are reasonable grounds to believe that the child is suffering or likely to suffer significant harm. In such circumstances, whilst of course the evidence necessary to establish those grounds must be presented to the court, the vast majority of the investigation will take place after the issue of proceedings – and indeed with input from all parties and oversight by the court.

If there is time, the decision whether to issue care proceedings will be taken at or discussed during the Initial Child Protection Conference. Where there are allegations of a criminal act, then the police will be automatic invitees to this and subsequent conferences so that they will be involved in the discussions, will inform the LA of the progress of the police investigation, and will be informed by the LA about the progress of its investigation.

All new care proceedings must usually be issued, in the first instance, in the Family Proceedings Court (FPC).[5]

---

[5]   Children (Allocation of Proceedings) Order 1991, SI 1991/1677, art.3(2), (3) (there are exceptions where existing proceedings are already underway in another court).

Step	Documents produced

They can be transferred up to the county court or to the High Court very swiftly, if appropriate. Where there are complex parallel care and criminal investigations or proceedings, it would be unusual for the case to remain at FPC level.

Emergency protection orders

An EPO can usually only be made in an FPC, and may be made where the court is satisfied that:

- *Emergency protection order is prepared by the court. Copies are provided to the applicant and respondent parties, and retained on court file*

(a)   there is reasonable cause to believe that the child is likely to suffer significant harm if the child is not removed to LA accommodation, or kept in the place in which the child is currently being accommodated;[6] or

(b)   the LA is frustrated in its urgent section 47 enquiries by being unreasonably refused access to a child.[7]

The EPO can only initially be made for a maximum of eight days, though it can be extended once for a period of up to seven days.[8]

When applying for an EPO the LA must file sufficient evidence to establish its case even if the investigation has barely begun. If a serious allegation has been made – by a child via a third party or by a medical professional, for instance – then the evidence at this stage may be little more than a statement from the social worker exhibiting the best available evidence of the allegation. An EPO can be made without notice to the respondent parents, provided the application is properly made and strict guidelines are observed by the court. The courts have emphasised the drastic nature of EPOs, and the need for compelling reasons to make them. The relevant case law sets out in helpful checklist form the procedural and evidential duties on any LA making this application, whether or not it is made with notice to the respondents (although there are yet further requirements for an application made without notice).[9]

---

[6]   Children Act 1989, s.44(1)(a).
[7]   Children Act 1989, s.44(1)(b).
[8]   Children Act 1989, s.45(1), (5), (6).
[9]   See *X County Council* v. *B (Emergency Protection Orders)* [2005] 1 FLR 341; *Haringey LBC* v. *C, E and another* [2005] 2 FLR 47; and *Re X (Emergency Protection Orders)* [2006] EWHC 510 (Fam).

Step	Documents produced

An application for an EPO is a discrete application, and the proceedings come to an end upon the expiry of the order. However, in many cases the LA will then make an application for a care order, upon which the FPC may give directions to progress the case in various ways, some of which may interest the police in a dual investigation. The court may give directions about:

(a) the contact allowed between the child and any named person;[10]

(b) the medical or psychiatric examination or other assessment of the child;[11]

(c) limiting such examination or assessment without a further direction from the court.[12]

Indeed, unless a specific direction is made in relation to contact, the LA is under a duty to allow the child reasonable contact with his/her parents or any person with whom the child was living when the order was made.

At this very early stage, therefore, the court will take control of the investigation insofar as it directly involves the child. If the police need to involve the child in their investigation – by interview, for instance, or by medical examination – or if they are concerned about contact taking place between the child and the accused, then at this early stage they must be ready to liaise closely with the LA to explain their position and explain their requirements in time for the EPO application. There will be very little time, as this application envisages (as the title makes clear) that there is an emergency situation to be dealt with. If there are already bail conditions regulating contact between the accused and the child, then early discussions between the LA and police are essential to prevent courts making different orders about essentially the same issue.

Interim care orders

Once care proceedings are issued a first hearing will take place within three days at which the court may make interim care or supervision orders until it is ready for the final hearing.[13] These interim care orders may be made

- *Statements will be filed by LA and, if time, responded to by all parties*

---

[10] Children Act 1989, s.44(6)(a).
[11] Children Act 1989, s.44(6)(b).
[12] Children Act 1989, s.44(8).
[13] The court's powers at the interim stages are defined by Children Act 1989, s.38.

Step	Documents produced

for an initial period of up to eight weeks and thereafter for a maximum of 28 days each time. If the respondent parents wish to contest the making of the order, a contested hearing will take place.

When making interim orders the court also has the power to make an order in relation to contact between the child and named adults.[14] Again, unless a specific direction is made in relation to contact, the LA is under a duty to allow the child reasonable contact with his or her parents or any person with whom the child was living when the order was made. Liaison between police and the LA about this issue is clearly vital.

The court may make directions regarding medical examination, psychiatric examination or other assessments of the child.[15] Again, liaison between police and the LA at this stage is vital.

The court will also consider any necessary transfer of the case to the county court, and other immediate matters.

- *Interim care or supervision order is prepared by the court together with any court directions. Copies are provided to the applicant and respondent parties and retained on court file*

Appointment of Guardian and solicitor

The court appoints a children's Guardian, who will appoint a solicitor to represent the child(ren) in the proceedings.

Evidence

During the course of the proceedings, evidence will be filed by all parties and copied to all parties.

The evidence before the court will comprise the evidence submitted by the LA, including its social work statements, chronology and care plan (a document setting out the LA's proposals for the child's long-term placement and any interim measures including proposed assessments and contact arrangements), the respondents' evidence in reply, the Guardian's report and any expert evidence.

If appropriate, the court may order an assessment of the child (a 'section 38(6) assessment') which requires an assessment of the parents and child in a Residential Assessment Unit or in the community, usually for a period of 6–12 weeks, to assess the parents' relationship with and ability to parent the child. A letter of instruction will be agreed between the parties and filed with the

- *Contact session notes*
- *School reports/ records*
- *Child protection conference minutes*
- *Medical reports*
- *Expert parenting assessment reports*
- *Psychiatric/ psychological assessments*
- *Risk assessments*

---

[14] Children Act 1989, s.34.
[15] Children Act 1989, s.38(6), (7), (8).

Step	Documents produced

court. Often an interim report will be filed, followed by a final report.

The process of selecting and instructing experts is an open one, usually conducted with input from all parties, and with the oversight of the court. No statement or report may be obtained from an expert without the prior permission of the court. A letter of instruction will be prepared, usually by agreement, and filed with the court. The reports of instructed experts must be disclosed to all parties and filed with the court, regardless of whether the contents are unhelpful to the instructing party.

The family practitioner's advice to a client will always be in favour of openness and honesty in the family proceedings, i.e. that the client should admit any past wrongs. This may seem anathema to the criminal practitioner, however, it is a fundamental principle of family proceedings that parents are able to demonstrate insight into social work concerns, and honestly to confront and address issues in their parenting which require improvement. If harm has been done to a child in the past, the court will be unlikely to accept that the parents can move on to rehabilitation and adequately protect that child in the future, unless there has been a frank acceptance of past wrongs.

Directions hearings

Directions hearings will take place in accordance with the Judicial Case Management Protocol/Public Law Outline. A Case Management Conference will take place early in the proceedings to identify the issues in the proceedings, establish the evidence required, and set a timetable towards a final hearing. Under the Public Law Outline, and advocates meeting and Issues Resolution Hearing will take place in order to narrow and resolve issues.

- *Court directions*

Additional hearings will be listed by the court if issues arise requiring directions.

Pre-hearing review

A pre-hearing review will take place shortly before the final hearing to confirm that all necessary evidence has been collected and that the proceedings are ready for final determination.

The evidence will include the social work statements, final care plan, respondents' evidence in reply, the Guardian's report, and all expert evidence.

Step	Documents produced

Final hearing

At the final hearing, the court is asked to make a final decision on the LA's application.

Any application for disclosure of documents to the police or CPS should be made at this stage before the proceedings conclude by the police or CPS.

Two-stage hearing

In some cases, the final hearing is 'split' into two parts: (i) a causation (fact-finding) hearing, and (ii) an 'outcome', or 'welfare', hearing (previously known as a 'disposal hearing'). This system is not encouraged in every case, but is useful where the court must first establish the nature, if any, of the harm caused to a child and the identity of the perpetrator(s) of the harm, before deciding in a stage 2 hearing how best to 'dispose' of the case (i.e. what final orders should be made). This two-stage process is almost inevitable in cases of alleged sexual or physical abuse.

In cases where the hearing is in two parts, the evidence filed for the fact-finding hearing will be factual information about what happened to the child in the past. Whilst expert evidence is admissible at this stage of the proceedings, such evidence is most likely to be medical evidence (in cases of alleged physical harm), or evidence interpreting a child's allegations of (usually) sexual abuse. It is unusual for psychiatric or psychological assessments of the parents to be admitted at this stage of the case; the court will expect direct evidence of the facts to be found, rather than evidence which could at most establish a general propensity to commit the act(s) alleged.[16]

At the stage 2 hearing, the court may dismiss the application, make a final care or supervision order in favour of the LA, or make any other order under the Children Act 1989 it considers suitable. Depending on the circumstances of the case, and the identity of those chosen to provide permanent care for the child, the court may be asked to deal with applications for a special guardianship order (placing the child with any non-parent, including a family member or former foster carer) or a placement order (which permits the LA to place the child with prospective adopters, if the child's 'care plan' is for

- *The final order will be drawn up by the court and served on all parties.*

A transcript of the hearing and/or judgment is not routinely prepared at public expense, unless there is to be an appeal, or the judge orders that the judgment should be publicly reported. In appropriate cases, the CPS may request judicial permission for transcription, provided that the costs are being met by an appropriate authority.

In the FPC, a written Statement of Reasons will be produced.

---

[16]   *Re CB and JB (Care Proceedings: Guidelines)* [1998] 2 FLR 211.

Step	Documents produced
adoption). The court must consider the proposals for contact between a child who cannot return to his or her family, and the child's birth family members.	

2.3 PRIVATE LAW CHILDREN ACT 1989 PROCEEDINGS ROUTE MAP

'Private law' Children Act proceedings include applications between individuals for 'section 8' orders for residence, contact, prohibited steps and specific issue orders, and also special guardianship orders under section 14A. The conduct of proceedings is set within the President's Private Law Framework and many are dealt with through dispute resolution processes involving Cafcass. Such meetings are a form of in-court conciliation and are not confidential.

Concurrent private law Children Act proceedings and criminal proceedings or investigations may arise in a variety of circumstances, for example:

(a)   where there are allegations of domestic violence between adults, to which children may have been directly or indirectly exposed;

(b)   where there are allegations of physical and/or sexual abuse of children by their parents or other person.

Step	Documents produced
Issue of application	
All C1 application forms are sent to Cafcass for screening as to indications of risk.	• *Application forms C1 (and C1A, if harm to child is alleged, including witnessing domestic violence)*
In urgent cases, an ex parte application may be brought and a short hearing may take place without notice. The court will then list an on notice hearing at the earliest opportunity to allow the respondent to be heard.	• *A statement from the applicant must be filed, attaching (if appropriate) medical or other supporting evidence*

Step	Documents produced
	• *An accurate record of the hearing must be taken by the applicant's solicitor*

Upon the issue of private law Children Act proceedings, most courts will list the application for a dispute resolution appointment. It is Cafcass's intention to provide an officer either at court, or in advance of the hearing, to assist the parties to try and enable agreement between the parties if possible. Practice varies in different courts as to the stage at which it is appropriate directly to involve the child. In some courts this is routinely done; in others not at all. Many schemes involve the Cafcass officer seeing the child out of court. In some courts, such as the Principal Registry of the Family Division, children who are over a certain age may be asked to attend court.

In cases where allegations of domestic violence between adults or child abuse arise, a risk assessment will need to have been completed before a decision as to the appropriateness of dispute resolution can be made. Dispute resolution is generally considered inappropriate in such cases. All parties must now complete a form C1A indicating whether there are any issues of harm to the child. A copy of all forms C1 and C1A are sent to Cafcass as a matter of routine, to allow Cafcass to carry out a risk assessment. Cafcass screens all C1 forms, and undertakes some background checks as to risk factors. The parties and the court should be alert to the earliest identification of such issues within private law proceedings. Where information in the application or arising during the screening process suggests there may be a risk of harm then full police checks will also be carried out. In cases where there appears to be a need to do so, the Cafcass officer has a statutory duty to complete a risk assessment. Where information suggests there is an ongoing risk of harm, Cafcass will make a referral to the LA under a protocol agreed following implementation of Adoption and Children Act 2002, s.120.

Pursuant to the guidance given by the Court of Appeal in the case of *Re L (Contact: Domestic Violence) Re V, Re M, Re H* [2000] 2 FLR 334, the parties and court should consider whether a forensic enquiry or 'finding of fact' hearing into the allegations of domestic violence or child abuse is necessary and appropriate within the context of

Step	Documents produced

determining, for example, a child's residence or arrangements for contact between the child(ren) and the non-resident parent.

The court may also need to consider whether to direct an investigation by the relevant LA into the child's circumstances, pursuant to Children Act 1989, s.37 where it appears to the court that the child may have suffered significant harm and a care or supervision order may be appropriate.

First hearing dispute resolution appointment (FHDRA)

A FHDRA will take place (save in cases where this is inappropriate, for example domestic violence cases).

In ordinary circumstances, a FHDRA will be listed by the court as soon as it receives an application. The length of time involved before a first appointment can be offered varies widely between courts, and generally ranges from two to eight weeks. The Private Law Programme states that the FHDRA should take place within four to six weeks.

A FHDRA may not be held if the matter has been commenced by way of an urgent ex parte application – for example, where an urgent prohibited steps or residence order is needed to protect a child from being removed from his or her carer. A FHDRA may also not be listed if the circumstances make it inappropriate – for example, if there has been violence between the parties.

The court is required to scrutinise all proposed orders, whether or not reached by consent. This is particularly important in cases involving domestic violence, as the court must ensure that the proposed arrangements are in the child's best interests and that any necessary safeguarding measures have been properly put in place.

Where Cafcass have been involved in early dispute resolution, the officer may provide a short written or oral report to the court. No court record is made of these proceedings, save for any order/directions made by the court, which are drawn up by the court and served on all parties to the proceedings. In the FPC, a written Statement of Reasons is produced.

Directions for the filing of evidence in preparation for a final hearing

If the matter is not resolved at the FHDRA, directions will be made for the filing of evidence in preparation for a final hearing

Step	Documents produced

Fact-finding hearing

If necessary, a fact-finding ('Re L') hearing will take place so that the court can make findings as to disputed allegations of domestic violence, which one party is relying on to prevent contact between the child and the alleged perpetrator.

The court will make findings and deliver a judgment.

- *Respondent's Schedule of Findings Sought*
- *Police disclosure*
- *Medical evidence*
- *Statements from supporting witnesses*
- *Expert evidence and interim reports from Cafcass or the LA*
- *Typed judgment or solicitor's note of ex tempore judgment.*

A transcript of the judgment may be applied for, provided that appropriate arrangements are made for payment of transcription costs.

- *Court directions*

Interim directions

The court will hold directions hearings, at which it will make directions so as to ensure that all necessary evidence is collected and filed with the court, prior to a final hearing taking place. Directions may include:

- listing contested matters for hearing, including interim fact-finding hearings;
- setting a timetable for the filing of evidence and a date for the final hearing;
- filing of additional evidence;
- seeking disclosure of police information in matters with concurrent police investigation or proceedings;

Step	Documents produced

- ordering a welfare report pursuant to Children Act 1989, s.7, from either Cafcass or the LA's children and social care department (usually where they are already involved with family);

- ordering a report pursuant to Children Act 1989, s.37 by the relevant LA, where it appears that a care or supervision order may be appropriate;

- ordering the obtaining of expert evidence, e.g. from an adult or child psychiatrist;

- listing the matters for further dispute resolution, or inviting the parties to attend mediation, although this is less likely in cases involving serious issues of domestic violence;

- in exceptional circumstances, making the child(ren) parties to the proceedings, usually also appointing a Guardian who will appoint a solicitor to represent the child(ren) on the Guardian's instructions, unless the child(ren) is/are capable of directly instructing his or her (or their) own solicitor.

Contested interim hearings

A contested interim hearing may be needed if an issue needs to be resolved, such as issues of interim contact. The court will usually hear oral evidence from parties and relevant witnesses and consider what, if any, findings of fact to make. The court will also consider what orders to grant in respect of the child(ren), and may then proceed to consider further directions and timetabling.

- *Typed judgment or solicitor's note of ex tempore judgment*
- *Court directions*

Pre-hearing review/final directions hearing

The court will list a pre-hearing review, or final directions hearing, before the date upon which the final hearing is to take place. The review will be timetabled to take place upon receipt of the section 7 or section 37 report from Cafcass or the LA, and of any other evidence. Usually the review hearing will take place a few weeks prior to the final hearing.

The court will enquire whether agreement has been reached to resolve the issues in dispute, or whether a contested final hearing remains necessary. Final directions may be given for trial.

- *Final evidence from each party and their witnesses*
- *Final Cafcass or LA (section 7 or section 37) report*
- *Any expert evidence*

Step	Documents produced

Final hearing

At a contested final hearing, the court will hear oral evidence from the parties and any relevant witnesses. The court will consider what, if any, findings of fact to make, and what orders to grant in respect of the child(ren).

After hearing the evidence and making the necessary findings on dispute issues, the court will either make a final order, or may take the view that 'no order' is appropriate. Orders may deal with a wide range of issues related to the upbringing of the child(ren), including residence, contact, prohibited steps, specific issues, special guardianship or leave to remove a child permanently from the jurisdiction of England and Wales.

- *The final order will be drawn up by the court and served on all parties.*

A transcript of the hearing and/or judgment is not routinely prepared at public expense, unless there is to be an appeal, or the judge orders that the judgment should be publicly reported. In appropriate other cases the CPS may request judicial permission for transcription, provided that the costs are being met by an appropriate authority.

Review hearing

In some cases, the court may, at the final hearing, consider it appropriate to list the matter for a further review. At this hearing the court will consider what, if any, further orders to grant in respect of child(ren), and what, if any, further hearings are appropriate.

- *Updating statements from parties*
- *Addendum section 7 or section 37 reports from Cafcass or the LA.*

31

2.4 FAMILY LAW ACT 1996 (PART IV) (NON-MOLESTATION/ OCCUPATION ORDERS) PROCEEDINGS ROUTE MAP

Part IV proceedings are private law proceedings brought between individuals in cases where violence or harassment, actual or threatened, arises between persons in familial-type relationships.[17] Applicants may seek a non-molestation order (injuncting the respondent from using or threatening violence or harassment against the applicant) and/or an occupation order (which determines each party's rights to occupy the family home).

Summary

Step	Documents produced
Issue of application	
The application is issued.	• *Application form FL401*
In urgent cases, an application is often made 'without notice'. The applicant must file a statement of evidence, which if appropriate should attach medical or other supporting evidence.	• *Notice to landlord/ mortgagee on form FL406*
An accurate record of the hearing must be taken by the applicant's solicitor.	• *Statement of applicant*
An order may be granted after a short hearing in front of the court. The court will then list a return date for an on notice hearing at the earliest opportunity to allow the respondent to be heard.	• *Solicitor's note of hearing*
	• *Court orders will be produced by the court and held on court file*
Service	
The applicant must arrange for the respondent to be personally served with a copy of the order and supporting evidence. The order will state the date of the return date.	• *Affidavit of Service from process server*
A copy of the order must be lodged with the police.	

---

[17] The Act sets out a comprehensive list as to the types of relationships covered.

Step	Documents produced

The final order must be served personally upon the respondent. If a power of arrest is attached to the order (i.e. a provision allowing the police to arrest a respondent discovered to have breached the order), then a copy of the order and an Affidavit of Service must lodged with the relevant police station. Powers of arrest can only be attached to occupation orders.

Return hearing

The return date provides the respondent with the first opportunity to attend before the court and put his or her position.

If the respondent does not attend the return hearing, the court may extend the order for a specified period.

If the respondent does attend the return hearing,[18] the application may be resolved by consent if the court is prepared to accept undertakings from the respondent, or mutual undertakings from both parties. The court should only accept an undertaking where it is satisfied that it is safe to do so.

If a contested hearing is required, it may take place the same day; alternatively, directions may be made timetabling to final hearing. The order will usually be extended in the interim. Interim directions may be made including:

- providing for the filing of additional evidence;
- seeking disclosure of police information, in any matter with concurrent police investigation or proceedings;
- listing matters for contested finding of facts hearing.

- *Undertakings can be formally taken from the parties, and copies kept on the court file and distributed to all parties*
- *Directions order will be drawn by the court and served on all parties.*

Final hearing

At a contested final hearing, the court will hear oral evidence from the parties and any relevant witnesses. The court will consider what, if any, findings of fact to make, what orders to grant, and the duration of the same.

Final evidence from each party and their witnesses, including a statement in reply from the respondent, and any supporting police or medical evidence.

[18] Public funding is often unavailable from the Legal Services Commission for respondents to non-molestation order applications, and respondents do not always attend return hearings.

Step	Documents produced

Orders available

Non-molestation orders usually prohibit the respondent from using or threatening violence against the applicant and any named children, or from harassing or molesting the applicant, or encouraging any other person to do so.

A non-molestation order may include a prohibition against the respondent coming within a specified distance of the applicant's home, the applicant and named children personally, and other specified locations such as the child's school (presuming that the respondent is already aware of the school's name and location).

Non-molestation orders and occupation orders must be expressed to endure for a specified period, with a stated expiry date. The duration of these orders is at the court's discretion, but in usual circumstances they are allowed to expire between 6 and 24 months, so as to allow the matter to be revisited by the court within a reasonable period of time.

A power of arrest may be attached to an occupation order. Since the introduction of the Domestic Violence, Crime and Victims Act 2004, a power of arrest cannot be attached to a non-molestation order. Instead, breach of a non-molestation order is a criminal offence.

Enforcement

If a power of arrest has been attached to an occupation order, and the respondent breaches the order, it may result in the respondent being arrested and brought by the police as soon as practicable to the court where committal proceedings will take place. If the police do not do so, the applicant can enforce the order by bringing committal proceedings.

Where a non-molestation order is breached, this is a criminal offence[19] and may be punishable by prosecution brought by the police.[20]

The final order will be drawn up by the court and served on all parties.

A transcript of the hearing and/or judgment is not routinely prepared at public expense, unless there is to be an appeal, or the judge orders that the judgment should be publicly reported. In appropriate other cases the CPS may request judicial permission for transcription, provided that the costs are being met by an appropriate authority.

---

[19] Domestic Violence, Crime and Victims Act 2004.
[20] Further detail can be found in: HMCS (2007) *Domestic Violence, A Guide to Civil Remedies and Criminal Sanctions* (revised March 2007).

CHAPTER 3

Sharing information

This chapter deals with the general principles surrounding disclosure of:

(a)   information; and

(b)   documents and evidence.

This chapter is divided into the following sections:

- general principles;
- obtaining and using information from criminal proceedings;
- obtaining and using information from family proceedings.

For the respective jurisdictions, each section will deal with the following commonly asked questions, as well as questions specific to each jurisdiction:

Q: What are the general principles which govern the sharing of information in this jurisdiction? What court rules exist?

Q: At what stages is it prejudicial/appropriate to share information?

Q: How does one go about seeking the information? Whom does one talk to? How does one go about finding out what is available, and who has it?

Q: When are joint case management hearings needed?

3.1   GENERAL PRINCIPLES

Before starting, practitioners are encouraged to follow these general principles:

- Establish communication with all other legal representatives. Keep a solicitors' information sheet (see Appendix 1) on file detailing the contact information for the parties and representatives in the concurrent proceedings, and ensure it is regularly updated.

- Stay in regular communication with the legal representatives in the concurrent proceedings.

- Agree to provide each other with regular updates as far as possible within the constraints of the client's instructions. Exchange police station notes and information regarding the status of proceedings, impending directions hearings, and the evidence obtained to date.

- Be respectful of each other's limitations: documents may not be capable of being shared, particularly care proceedings documentation. However, be cooperative in your approach: if a formal application needs to be made, assist the other parties in understanding how this might be done.

- When liaising with the 'other' representative of your own client (i.e., in liaison between the care and criminal solicitors acting for a parent), be aware of the circumstances in which 'Chinese walls' are prudent. Care solicitors are obliged, once they have received information, to disclose it into the care proceedings. Once the local authority (LA) receives it, there is a likelihood that the police will become aware of it. Do not, therefore, share information with your client's care solicitor if the effect of doing so is not in your client's interests.

- Be alert to ongoing assessments proposed in care proceedings, as they may impact on sentencing decisions in concurrent criminal proceedings.

- Always be alert to, and keep under review, contact issues, which will impact upon sentencing and bail decisions (and vice versa: sentences may impact upon contact arrangements).

3.2 OBTAINING AND USING INFORMATION FROM CRIMINAL PROCEEDINGS

LAs, family practitioners and Cafcass may often have a legitimate interest in gaining information about, or access to documents produced in, a criminal investigation or prosecution. Practitioners should give particular consideration to seeking:

(a) *information* about the timescales for the conclusion of the investigation, decision to charge and/or the timing of prosecution; the nature of evidence obtained by the police; and bail conditions, particularly those involving children; and

(b) *documentation* including records of interview, expert medical reports, forensic evidence, photographs of injuries or crime scenes, and witness statements taken by the police (from family, friends, neighbours, emergency service officers and other witnesses not usually spoken to by the LA).

Q: What are the general principles which govern the sharing of information in this jurisdiction? What court rules exist?

Information/documents disclosed during trial

In contrast to the family court, there are no court rules governing access to documents filed in criminal proceedings. Criminal proceedings take place in open court, and there are no general statutory restrictions upon the reporting or sharing of information once it has been used in a criminal trial. However, all information/documentation will be covered by the general law of confidence, and consequently these documents should not be filed into the family proceedings without the permission of the Crown Prosecution Service (CPS).

Obtaining information/documentation before trial

Most family practitioners and LAs, however, will be interested in accessing information before trial. Family proceedings often run on a shorter timetable than criminal investigations, and information may be required whilst the criminal proceedings are at an earlier stage. In some cases, the family proceedings may reach final hearing before police investigations have concluded or charges have been laid.

There are no written rules governing the ability of the police/CPS to share information in their possession prior to being obliged by the Criminal Procedure and Investigations Act 1996 to provide disclosure to the defence. The general principle, however, is that the police/CPS will decline to share information if it would be prejudicial to their investigation to do so, or would be in breach of the Data Protection Act 1998 or European Convention on Human Rights principles such as Art.8 (right to privacy).

The information received by the defence from the CPS by way of 'advance information' is provided on the implied condition that it has been provided for the sole purpose of informing the defence of the elements of the prosecution's case. The general law of confidence requires that the defence should not share this information with others, as it will otherwise lead to the potential tainting of other witnesses' evidence. Consequently, these documents should not be filed into the family proceedings without the permission of the CPS.

Q: At what stages is it prejudicial/appropriate to share information?

It will be a matter for the police to determine whether the sharing of information in their possession is likely to be prejudicial to their investigations.

As a general principle, however, the police will be reluctant to share information prior to the CPS making a decision to charge. Once the CPS has charged the suspect, the suspect will be entitled to 'advance information' and thus will come into possession of the prosecution's key evidence in any event.

Q: How does one go about seeking the information? Whom does one talk to? How does one go about finding out what is available, and who has it?

Prior to charge, enquiries may be made of the investigating officer. Post-charge, enquiries may be made of the allocated CPS lawyer.

Exchange of information

There is no prescribed mechanism for the exchange of *information*, as opposed to *documentation* (dealt with below). In practice, the exchange of such information is thus largely haphazard. For example, information may come to the family courts from the party who is under police investigation, or through informal dialogue between the criminal and family representatives acting for the defendant. In addition, there is no reliable prescribed mechanism by which a defendant's bail conditions, or any variations thereof, are disclosed to the family court. It is therefore important, if possible:

(a) to identify a named network of personnel with conduct of the criminal investigation and family proceedings, together with their direct contact details;

(b) so far as is possible at any given stage in the police investigation, to encourage regular network liaison, with prompt exchange of agreed documentation and discussion as to timescales for the resolution of disputed disclosure, with regular updates to be exchanged in this regard; and

(c) to ensure that 'informal' exchange of information is recorded accurately and copied to all appropriate network members.

Exchange of documentation

Practitioners should always begin with informal liaison, following the procedures set out in the ACPO Police/Family Disclosure Protocol, ensuring that the request is made early enough to allow sufficient time for the police to respond (usually within five working days).[1] The ACPO Protocol is intended to apply to records held by all branches of the police, and in all types of family proceedings. However, each of the 43 police forces has discretion to implement the protocol in a way that best suits local practice, and implementation may therefore vary. Contact should be made with the central Domestic Abuse Coordinator in each force area, who will have knowledge of the local practice and relevant contact persons. Information supplied by the police in pursuance of this protocol is subject to certain implicit undertakings on the part of the parties and their legal representatives – unless directed otherwise by the court. For example, any material disclosed is to be used only for the purposes of, and preparation for, concurrent family proceedings. Material is to be kept confidential and copying to be kept to a minimum to avoid unnecessary proliferation of sensitive material.

Where a protocol request has been unsuccessful, an application may be made to the family court judge, on notice to the police, for an order directing the relevant police authority to disclose documents within a defined period. Such applications should normally be made using a witness summons to a named responsible officer, requiring the police to attend court with the material. The care judge will consider the scope of the request, and may make an order. If the police are not represented at

---

[1] The protocol and forms are attached in Appendix 2, and can also be obtained in electronic format by accessing this guide online (**www.family-justice-council.org.uk**).

the hearing, they must be given liberty to apply to challenge or vary the order. If the police seek to refuse disclosure, the court will balance the public interest in maintaining the document's confidentiality (the disclosure of which may prejudice or inhibit a pending investigation or prosecution), against the public interest in ensuring that the family court has access to all material which may assist it in protecting the best interests of the child.

For a useful guide as to standard variable directions granted by the family court in relation to the disclosure of police material, see Annex D to the Police/Family Disclosure Protocol.

In care proceedings, the issue of disclosure falls into two stages – first, that of disclosure to the LA; and second, whether disclosure should be made by the LA to the other parties. In practice this two-stage process rarely occurs: routinely the court will direct the categories of document that should be served on the LA, who will copy the documents to the other parties. Where the two-stage process is followed, the issue of whether the LA should disclose to the other parties is decided in accordance with the usual public interest immunity (PII) arguments presented in respect of LA records (see Chapter 8).

In private law family proceedings, disclosure will ordinarily be made to the court, rather than an individual party. Any documents filed in the proceedings are to be distributed to all parties, save in exceptional circumstances.[2]

Usually the issue for the police is not whether to object to disclosure in principle, but the appropriate timing of disclosure, i.e. when will disclosure no longer pose any risk to the progress of the criminal investigation? Such issues are most acute when the defendant is one or both of the child's parents who are parties to the civil process and thus likely recipients of any disclosed documents.

It is recommended that, as best practice, the police/CPS should provide regular 'progress reports' which all parties in the family proceedings may see, so as to enable the court and parties to understand what information the police hold, what can be disclosed, and when it can be disclosed. If there are categories of information too sensitive to disclose at a particular time, then in very general terms the court and the parties can be told this, and given an idea of when the police/CPS would be likely to agree to disclosure. Obviously if there is a real issue to be tried,

---

[2] Family Proceedings Rules 1991, rule 4.17.

then the police will be expected to file a statement setting out as much as is appropriate on this matter. Whether the police provide information through routine progress reports or in a statement, it is very important to everyone in the civil process to understand what evidence is sensitive at what stage and why.

Q: When are joint case management hearings needed?

Joint case management directions hearings may be useful wherever there are concurrent criminal and family proceedings and issues arise as to disclosure of information, or mutually convenient timetabling.[3]

Criminal Procedure Rules 2005, SI 2005/384, rule 3.2(1) requires the court to further the overriding objective, which includes, at rule 1.1(2)(e), dealing with the case efficiently and expeditiously by actively managing the case; and, at rule 1.1(2)(g)(iii), dealing with the case in ways that take into account the needs of other cases. Question 33 of the prescribed plea and case management hearing (PCMH) form requires details of any concurrent family proceedings to be entered on that form. This will allow the Designated Family Judge to be alerted. In fulfilling the court's duty of case management in Part 3 of the Criminal Procedure Rules, an order for a joint case management hearing may be made.

Q: What is the role of Cafcass in obtaining a list of criminal convictions or other relevant police information?

An officer of Cafcass is always appointed to represent the interests of the child in care proceedings (as Children's Guardian), and in private law Children Act proceedings will often be tasked with preparing a section 7 report to investigate residence/contact or a specific issue relevant to the child(ren). Information held by the police may be shared with the family court via the Cafcass officer in his or her report. Cafcass have entered into a national protocol with the police to allow the sharing of information relevant to the protection of children.

The relevant previous criminal convictions of the parties to the proceedings should normally be outlined in the Cafcass report. In particular, in accordance with the Cafcas protocol, the police, upon receiving a written request form from Cafcass, should supply information relevant

---

[3] See Chapter 4.

to the protection of the children and the safety of adults involved in the care of, or having contact with, such children including incidents dealt with by the Domestic Violence Unit, the Child Protection Unit or other relevant police information.

3.3 OBTAINING AND USING INFORMATION FROM FAMILY PROCEEDINGS

The police/CPS may have a legitimate interest in obtaining either information or documentation in respect of family proceedings, as such information may prove crucial to the decision to charge, the choice of charge, the setting of bail conditions, the handling of witnesses (including any special measures needed), the credibility of witnesses (including being aware of inconsistent previous statements) and the admissibility of bad character and hearsay evidence.

The categories of documents most frequently sought by the police are:

- expert reports;
- parties' statements;
- transcripts of evidence (especially if any admissions have been made); and
- the transcript of the judgment where findings have been made, or not made.

Q: **What are the general principles which govern the sharing of information in this jurisdiction? What court rules exist?**

Family proceedings are held in private, and are therefore confidential. *Orders* made by the court are not protected, and may be disclosed to any person provided that the order is not published to the wider population (as this may amount to identifying the child as the subject of current Children Act proceedings, which is a criminal offence).[4]

---

[4]   It is a criminal offence to publish information to the public at large, or any section of the public, which identifies a child as the subject of proceedings under either the Children Act 1989 or the Adoption and Children Act 2002: Children Act 1989, s.97(2).

Exchange of documentation

Any documents filed in family proceedings are confidential and may only be disclosed in accordance with the Family Proceedings Rules (FPR) 1991, SI 1991/1247, or with the permission of the court.[5] It may be a contempt of court[6] to disclose information contrary to the Rules.

The FPR 1991 allow for all filed documents to be disclosed to the following persons:

- the parties and their legal representatives;
- professional legal advisers not instructed in the proceedings (e.g. legal advisers who provide advice for the Citizens' Advice Bureau or other such agencies);
- Cafcass and Cafcass Cymru or an LA preparing a section 7 report;
- the Legal Services Commission;
- an expert whose instruction has been authorised by the court; and
- a professional acting in furtherance of the protection of children.[7]

'A professional acting in furtherance of the protection of children' is defined at rule 10.20A(5) to include:

(a)   an officer of a local authority exercising child protection functions;

(b)   a police officer who is –

  (i)   exercising powers under s.46 of the Children Act 1989, or

  (ii)   serving in a child protection unit or paedophile unit of a police force;

(c)   any professional attending a child protection conference or review in relation to a child who is the subject of the proceedings to which the information relates; or

(d)   an officer of the NSPCC.

It is also possible for other persons listed in the Rules to receive certain documents, but only the documents specified in the Rules, from specified

5   FPR 1991, rule 10.20A.
6   Administration of Justice Act 1960, s.12.
7   FPR 1991, rule 10.20A(2).

people, and only for specified purposes. Where a recipient of documents wishes to use them for any other purpose, an application must be made to the family court. For example:

- *a police officer* may be given *the text or summary of the whole or part of a judgment given in the proceedings,* but only *for the purpose of a criminal investigation*;

- *a member of the Crown Prosecution Service* may also receive *the text or summary of the whole or part of a judgment given in the proceedings,* but only *for the purpose of enabling the CPS to discharge its functions under any enactment.*[8]

An application for access to documents must be made to the judge in the proceedings. In care cases, the police often ask the LA to make an application on their behalf. It is, however, recommended that the better course of action is for the police/CPS to make their own application. The prosecuting authority will know what is wanted and why it is relevant to the prosecution's purposes. The LA is not a limb of the police, and it is not helpful for the respondent parents to perceive them as such.

Exchange of information

The restrictions above do not apply to the sharing of *information*. There is a positive duty on the LA in civil proceedings to liaise with other relevant authorities such as the police. There is no bar upon the exchange of information between those engaged in the child protection process: a social worker can, and indeed ought to, inform the police of admissions made to him or her by a parent which are relevant to a joint investigation.

In the exchange of information, it is critical for good lines of communication to exist from the outset between a named LA lawyer and either the officer in the case or a named CPS representative. Where possible, a running record of exchanges should be kept alongside the regular progress reports suggested above detailing the progress of the criminal investigation – even in the most general of terms where information is especially sensitive.

---

[8]   FPR 1991, rule 10.20A(3).

Q: At what stages is it prejudicial/appropriate to share information?

There is far less likely to be any issue of timing in respect of disclosure from family proceedings into the criminal arena. After all, anything filed in the civil proceedings will, save in rare circumstances, have already been disclosed to all parties including the parents.

Q: How does one go about seeking the information? Whom does one talk to? How does one go about finding out what is available, and who has it?

In relation to documents which have not been filed with the family court, the national ADSS/CPS/ACPO Protocol makes provision for applications by the police/CPS for access to the LA's files.[9] Requests should be made in accordance with the protocol in those areas in which it has been implemented. Local CPS or LA lawyers will be able to advise as to whether implementation has occurred locally.

In relation to any documents already filed in family proceedings, an approach may be made to the LA (in care proceedings), or the parties' solicitors, to seek information in general terms as to what documents exist. The police/CPS should then make a decision as to whether or not to make an application to the family court to see the documents.

On such an application, the court will attempt in each case to strike a balance between the importance of maintaining confidentiality in the family case, the interests of the child (which are not paramount in this context) and the public interest in making relevant information available for other proceedings. Usually, where there is a concurrent criminal case, the application by the police will be granted – especially, perhaps, where the police are expected by the civil court to make similar disclosure in return.

The defendant has the protection of Children Act 1989, s.98(2) so that no statement or admission made by the defendant in the care proceedings shall be admissible in evidence against him or her in criminal proceedings.[10]

---

[9] See Appendix 2.
[10] See Chapter 7.

Q: When are joint case management hearings needed?

Joint case management directions hearings may be useful wherever there are concurrent criminal and family proceedings and issues arise as to disclosure of information, or mutually convenient timetabling.[11]

Q: What principles are applied to an application to the family court for police access to documents?

The court will exercise its discretion by balancing the importance of confidentiality and its importance in encouraging openness in family proceedings, against the public interest in seeing justice administered where a crime has been committed.[12]

The key factors to be weighed will include:

- the child's and the family's interests in maintaining privacy;

- the public interest in avoiding deterring openness in Children Act cases from parents, family members, health and education professionals;

- the particular public interest in encouraging frankness from perpetrators of child abuse (as enshrined by the privilege contained in Children Act 1989, s.98(2));

- the interests of the administration of justice, including the need to ensure a fair trial in criminal proceedings;

- the interests of children generally, including that perpetrators of child abuse be brought to justice;

- the gravity of the alleged offence;

- the relevance of the material to the purpose for which disclosure is sought;

- the prospect of rehabilitation of the child to his or her parents' care.[13]

---

[11] See Chapter 4.

[12] *Re D (Minors) (Wardship: Disclosure)* [1994] 1 FLR 346.

[13] See *Re X (Disclosure of Information)* [2001] 2 FLR 440; *Re R (Children: Disclosure)* [2003] 1 FCR 193; *Re EC (Disclosure of Material)* [1996] 2 FLR 725; *Re M (Care Proceedings: Disclosure: Human Rights)* [2001] 2 FLR 1316; *Re AB (Care Proceedings: Disclosure of Medical Evidence to Police)* [2002] EWHC (Fam) 2198.

CHAPTER 4

Joint case management hearings

4.1 BACKGROUND

Concurrent proceedings involving criminal and family issues involve
not only different jurisdictions but also different parties, different court
buildings and different tiers of court. There may, however, often be
considerable overlap between proceedings, and strong grounds for
maintaining liaison between the two. Joint case management hearings
are an opportunity to bring the parties and legal representatives in
concurrent criminal and civil proceedings together. The precise format
of the hearing will vary between local regions, where different practices
will be adopted based on the available judiciary and the 'tickets' issued
to them.

The problem has been recognised for more than 10 years and was, in
particular, raised in the 1993/4 Annual Report of the Children Act
Advisory Committee (CAAC). A sub-group of the CAAC produced a
working model for joint directions which it was agreed would be piloted
in Liverpool (as a large combined court centre) and Norwich (as a small
centre). Since then a scheme has developed between the Royal Courts of
Justice and London Crown Courts and individual initiatives have been
tried elsewhere.

The number of cases which have been covered by these schemes is small
and none has been formally evaluated. However, anecdotal evidence
suggests two broad conclusions. First, where the schemes have been
used, the advantage of having everyone involved together at the same
time has been found to be helpful, especially to deal with specific problems mentioned below. The only real reservation expressed has been the
time that these hearings sometimes take when criminal practitioners
have been kept waiting whilst complex family directions are given.
Second, their operation has been greatly restricted by the sheer practical

difficulty of courts being made aware in good time of the existence of concurrent proceedings. This has proved so even in schemes limited to public law and criminal proceedings involving the same child and only the county court and Crown Court.

A number of circumstances have combined to provide fresh opportunity to re-visit this procedure, and promote a consistent case management approach. The advent of a Unified Court Administration, the development of case management techniques in the Crown Court and the more open flow of information about children between agencies offer a new prospect of working across jurisdictions. Moreover, there is no reason in principle why this should not extend to all tiers of court and cover private as well as public law issues.

Under the Liverpool/Norwich systems, the key informant was the local authority solicitor who would know of both sets of proceedings and was tasked with keeping others informed. It simply did not work, although the reason for this was not clear. The scheme was initially limited to public law cases in the county court and criminal cases in the Crown Court. What happened in practice was either that the parties volunteered the existence of other proceedings so as to obtain joint directions, or (more usually) it was picked up by a judge either allocating cases or taking a directions hearing. In short, where the system worked, it worked because judges were alert to it and parties were willing to cooperate.

4.2 PURPOSE

There are, it must be recognised, a number of factors that tend to work against prompt joint directions hearings. These include: communications between magistrates' court, county court and Crown Court; an increasing degree of specialisation in the legal profession which means that no one lawyer may be involved in both sets of proceedings; fewer judges ticketed for both family and serious sexual offences in crime; fewer combined court centres; and, particularly where death or serious injury to a child occurs, a conflict between the pace of the local authority's need to protect, and the police duty to investigate. It is not always a simple matter to dovetail the separate proceedings, especially as one set might not even have begun when directions are first being given in the other.

On the other hand, real advantages can be gained from the process of joint directions. Experience suggests that joint directions hearings can provide a valuable opportunity to consider the following three specific matters:

(a) coordinated timetabling of proceedings with a view, where possible, to disposal of criminal proceedings first;

(b) the coordination of expert evidence to prevent unnecessary duplication and to ensure that experts have all available information; and

(c) to resolve issues of information sharing both within and across the concurrent proceedings.

It is in these areas particularly that real benefit is to be found. This may be as applicable to the magistrates' court as to the higher courts.

It has been demonstrated that the judicial role is the critical one not only in managing joint directions but in the identification of cases for which joint directions may be suitable. This must involve, as a minimum, both the existence of other proceedings being a standard question in all case management hearings and the copying across of orders between jurisdictions so that any subsequent judge is alerted to the question. So far these schemes have not involved the magistrates' court. Where both cases are proceeding there, no real difficulties need arise but where one is in a higher court, additional issues of communication, transfer, committal and delay will need to be addressed.

4.3 PROCEDURE

Prompted by the Family-Criminal Interface Committee, the Family Rules Committee and Criminal Procedure Rules Committee have both been working on the procedural details and formal arrangements.

The Criminal Procedure Rules Committee has now made changes to the case management forms, so as to ensure that the potential need for a joint case management hearing is considered at an early stage. All levels of the family and criminal judiciary have been informed of the format and benefits of joint hearings, and practitioners can expect such hearings to increasingly feature.

Some local regions have adopted Practice Directions, or local protocols. Enquiries should be made to the local Court Manager, who in conjunction with the local Resident Criminal Judge will be able to advise whether a local arrangement has been put in place. In other areas, the absence of a Practice Direction in local regions should not discourage the use of joint hearings wherever they may be useful. The judiciary and practitioners should be alert to the benefits of joint hearings, and consider whether a hearing would be useful in any case where there are concurrent or anticipated family and criminal proceedings.

Experience suggests that different difficulties arise in different areas; a large combined court centre presents far fewer problems than would be encountered in a widespread rural area like the West Country or much of Wales. We would, however, encourage adoption of the following general principles:

(a)   that every tribunal should be alert to the possibility of concurrent or anticipated proceedings in another jurisdiction;

(b)   that information about those proceedings should be readily available, especially in relation to orders which have already been made;

(c)   that this should be a matter considered at any directions hearing;

(d)   that a joint directions hearing should be convened unless the court is satisfied that such a hearing is unnecessary, bearing in mind that not every case of concurrent proceedings will require a joint directions hearing.

As to conduct of the joint directions hearing itself, experience suggests a number of matters which ought to be taken into account:

(a)   the taking of these hearings should be concentrated in as few judges or magistrates (and advisors) as possible so as to build up both experience and consistency of practice;

(b)   parties should be expected to deal with any relevant matter, but in particular:

(i)   coordinated timetabling (which will usually mean having access to both diary managers);

(ii)   disclosure and information sharing issues; and

(iii) expert evidence (which should include identified experts, their willingness to act within the court timetable and their availability as witnesses if required);

(c)   a fixed adjourned directions hearing should be set before the same tribunal if any matters common to both proceedings remain outstanding;

(d)   some proceedings will be heard in public, and some in private. Family proceedings remain in chambers, and non-parties (i.e. the prosecution) will not usually be admitted without the permission of the judge and the agreement of all parties. Generally this latter point throws up few practical problems. The plea will be taken in open court. The court can then sit in private and, if necessary, resume in public if orders and reasons for them in criminal proceedings need to be announced.

This guidance is not intended to consider the extent to which the judge may continue as trial judge in either or both jurisdictions. It is important to identify the benefits and disadvantages of any such proposal.

CHAPTER 5

Pre-trial therapy

5.1 INTRODUCTION

This subject has been the source of much misconception and confusion. The clear guidelines issued by the Crown Prosecution Service (CPS) indicate that there is no blanket ban on prosecuting a case where a child or adult has received therapy prior to trial. Guidance does, however, require that care is taken as to the *types* of therapy used. It is the nature of the therapy that is a key issue, rather than the occurrence itself and many forms of therapy will have no adverse impact on the criminal case.

It is important to distinguish here between therapy and other forms of work with child witnesses, including witness preparation and emotional support. Both of the latter are perfectly acceptable. This chapter relates only to issues to be considered before embarking on therapeutic work with a child.

The best interests of the vulnerable or intimidated witness are paramount when deciding whether, when and in what form therapeutic help is given. Whether a witness should receive therapy before the criminal trial is not a decision for the police or CPS and those involved in the prosecution have no authority to prevent any witness from receiving therapy. It is for the witness and their carers, in conjunction with the professional agencies providing support, to decide whether or not to undertake therapy.

The police and CPS must, however, be made aware that therapy is proposed, is being undertaken or has been undertaken. The nature of the therapy should be explained so that consideration can be given to whether or not the provision of such therapy is likely to impact on the criminal case.

Where a witness has received therapy, prosecutors must then obtain an assurance that the witness did not, in the therapy session(s), say anything inconsistent with the statement made by the witness to the police.

Records of therapy (which include videos and tapes as well as notes) and other contacts with the witness must be maintained so that they can be produced, if required by the court.

5.2 TIMING OF THERAPEUTIC WORK

Delaying therapy, pending the outcome of a criminal trial, for fear that the witness' evidence could be considered tainted and the prosecution lost, conflicts with the need to ensure that child and vulnerable adult victims are able to receive, as soon as possible, immediate and effective treatment to assist their recovery. In the context of this potential conflict, the following matters are relevant:

- many victims express the wish to see their abuser convicted and punished;

- there is a wider public interest in ensuring that abusers are brought to justice to prevent further abuse; and

- all accused persons are entitled to a fair trial.

It therefore follows that both care professionals and forensic investigators have a mutual interest in ensuring, wherever possible, that witnesses who receive therapy prior to a criminal trial are regarded as able to give a reliable testimony.

The evidence of a child in criminal proceedings is taken at the earliest opportunity by way of video interview (sometimes called the 'Achieving Best Evidence' (ABE) or 'memorandum' interview). Once the statement or video recorded interview is complete, it should be possible for appropriate counselling and therapy to take place.

Therapy is not usually encouraged before that stage because of the risk that it might be considered to affect or taint the witness' evidence and the likelihood of a prosecution being jeopardised can therefore be greater. However, if therapy is already underway, a decision as to how to proceed may be best made after discussion at a multi-disciplinary meeting, which includes the therapist.

If there is a demonstrable need for the provision of therapy and it is possible that the therapy will prejudice the criminal proceedings, consideration may need to be given to abandoning those proceedings in the interests of the witness' well being. The prosecutor will need to consider the importance of the witness' evidence, whether there is any sign that therapy has already tainted their evidence, and the wider public interest, before proceedings are abandoned. In order that such consideration can be given, it is essential that information regarding therapy is communicated to the prosecutor.

Alternatively, there will be some witnesses for whom it will be preferable to delay therapy until after the criminal case has been heard, to avoid the benefits of the therapy being undone.

5.3 CONFIDENTIALITY

The issue raised by any discussions undertaken prior to the criminal trial, including therapy, is whether the process can affect – that is to say, undermine – the actual or perceived reliability of that witness' evidence and the weight the jury will attach to it. This will depend on a number of factors, such as the circumstances in which the discussions take place.

Prosecutors may need to be made aware of the contents of the therapy sessions as well as other details when considering whether or not to prosecute and their duties of disclosure.

Records of therapy (including videos, tapes and notes) and other contacts with the witness must therefore be maintained so that they can be produced if required by the court. They should include, in the case of therapy, details of those persons present and the content and length of the therapy sessions. It is not expected that verbatim written records will be kept.

Because of the recognition that maintaining a client's trust is central to the provision of therapy, it will usually only be appropriate to breach confidentiality in compliance with a court order. Those aspects of the therapy that have no material relevance to criminal proceedings should not have to be disclosed. However, the issue of relevance may need to be reviewed at different stages of the criminal case, as more becomes known about the prosecution and defence cases. Confidentiality therefore cannot be guaranteed in advance. Consequently, it is important that an understanding is reached with the witness and/or the witness' carers at the outset of therapy, of the circumstances under which material obtained during treatment may be required to be disclosed.

5.4 EXAMPLES OF TYPES OF THERAPEUTIC WORK

Some types of therapeutic work are more likely to be seen as prejudicial and thereby undermine the perception of a witness' credibility and reliability or to influence a witness' memory of events or the account they give. Preparation for court and carefully planned preventative work which does not focus upon past abuse presents far less of a problem than interpretive psychodynamic psychotherapy. Hence, there is a spectrum of evidential risk to the criminal trial which should be considered.

The least problematic aspect of therapy will focus on improving self-esteem and self-confidence, often using cognitive/behavioural techniques. Other issues which might be addressed include the reduction of distress about the impending legal proceedings and the treatment of associated emotional and behavioural disturbance that does not require the rehearsal of abusive events.

Interpretive psychotherapy may present evidential problems even if carefully conducted. The professional background and training of the therapist, the provision of adequate supervision arrangements, the appropriateness and robustness of the policies of the agency providing therapy will all help to obviate problems.

Certain therapeutic approaches very definitely present problems so far as evidential reliability is concerned. These would include hypnotherapy, psychodrama, regression techniques and unstructured groups.

The best interests of the vulnerable or intimidated witness are paramount when deciding whether, when and in what form therapeutic help is given.

Full guidance can be found in *Provision of Therapy for Child Witnesses Prior to a Criminal Trial (Practice Guidance)* published in 2001 and in *Provision of Therapy for Vulnerable or Intimidated Adult Witnesses Prior to a Criminal Trial (Practice Guidance)* published in 2002. Both of these documents can be found at **www.cps.gov.uk** and **www.homeoffice.gov.uk**.

CHAPTER 6

Pre-trial contact

In any case involving a child there will inevitably be decisions to be made regarding contact between the child and family members and other significant persons. In cases involving concurrent family and criminal matters, where there has been possible sexual or physical abuse of a child, contact between a child victim and an accused relative will always involve difficult choices. In other cases involving children as non-victims, there will remain difficult choices.

6.1 GENERAL PRINCIPLE

It is an accepted tenet of child law that contact between a child and absent parent(s) is generally in the child's best interests. As long as a child is safe from harm, such contact should generally be encouraged so as to preserve attachments and preserve the child's sense of identity.

6.2 PUBLIC LAW CASES

Where there is a suspicion that children have been harmed, the local authority (LA) is likely to seek to restrict contact between the child and the suspected perpetrator. The LA may ask that agreements be signed by parents, requiring that the suspected perpetrator leave the family home and restricting contact with him or her. If the agreement is breached and contact nevertheless takes place, the LA may take further action, such as removing the children.

Following the issue of proceedings, the LA will usually seek to facilitate some form of supervised contact between the child and the child's parents and/or significant extended family members. Liaison may be required with police where an investigation or prosecution is pending. There is no general principle preventing contact prior to criminal trial; there may, however, be good reason to suspend contact for a short period until after an Achieving Best Evidence (ABE) interview can be arranged so as to ensure that the child's evidence is not tainted. Once the interview has taken place, any concerns regarding the tainting of the child's evidence should be capable of being met by supervision arrangements.

All decisions must, however, be child centred; if it appears to the LA that contact is not in the child's best interests, or is likely to cause further trauma to the child, contact may be terminated. The LA must remain alert to its duty under Children Act 1989, s.34 and must seek the court's permission if it seeks to prevent contact between a child and any family member for more than seven days (Children Act 1989, s.34).

The police/Crown Prosecution Service (CPS) must be informed of any contact arrangements made, so as to ensure that bail conditions are set consistently, and any particular concerns regarding potential tainting of evidence dealt with.

6.3 DOMESTIC VIOLENCE AND PRIVATE LAW CASES

The general principle in favour of contact with non-resident parents has been modified in recent years owing to a greater understanding of the harm children suffer from witnessing domestic violence between their parents. The Court of Appeal has given clear guidelines as to the approach to be adopted in such cases,[1] but the presence of domestic violence in itself is not a bar to a contact order being made in favour of a violent parent. In ordering contact, the court can ensure safeguards are in place. Where direct contact takes place, a range of safeguarding measures can be put in place, such as using neutral contact centre venues and having a third party assist in collecting the child, to avoid the risk of the victim being required to meet their ex-partner.

Concurrent criminal and family proceedings may raise difficulties. Where there are bail conditions forbidding an accused from attending the family property, care must be taken to ensure that the family court does not simultaneously grant a conflicting contact order. Conversely,

---

[1]   See *Re L, M, V and H* [2001] 2 WLR 339; [2000] 4 All ER 609; [2000] 2 FLR 334.

where the criminal court is considering bail conditions, it is important that the existence of any pre-existing order (either granting, or refusing, direct contact) is taken into account. Where bail is being set by the court, legal representatives of the CPS and defendant should take steps to ensure that the court is fully informed of any existing family court orders; where an unrepresented defendant is being given police bail at the police station, efforts should be made by the police to obtain all relevant information as to any concurrent proceedings or orders.

CHAPTER 7

Children Act 1989, s.98(2)

7.1 PROVISION OF s.98(2)

Section 98 of the Children Act 1989 provides:

(1) In any proceedings in which a court is hearing an application for an order under Part IV or V, no person shall be excused from –

    (a) giving evidence on any matter; or

    (b) answering any question in the course of giving evidence,

on the ground that doing so might incriminate him or his spouse or civil partner of an offence.

(2) A statement or admission made in such proceedings shall not be admissible in evidence against the person making it or his spouse or civil partner in proceedings for an offence other than perjury.

'Statement or admission' has been interpreted as including: witness statements filed in the proceedings; statements or admissions made to the Guardian during the course of his or her investigation;[2] and any statement made to an expert during his assessment.[3]

The intention of s.98(2) is to protect a parent from criminal proceedings based upon admissions made in care proceedings. However, s.98(2) does not provide absolute protection.

As discussed in section 3.3 of Chapter 3 above, the court may still give leave for documents to be disclosed to a third party, including the police. Once the police have received those documents, 'there is nothing

---

1   *Oxfordshire County Council* v. *P* [1995] 1 FLR 552.
2   *Oxfordshire County Council* v. *P* [1995] 1 FLR 552.
3   *A Chief Constable* v. *A County Council and others* [2003] 2 FCR 385.

in the terms of s.98 which inhibits further questioning [by the police] certainly before the suspected person is charged with the offence'.[4] It is important, therefore, that a client is advised during a police interview that the police may put to them statements made in the care proceedings, and that if the client then accepts those statements they will form part of the admissible interview. If the client does not adopt, or makes no comment on, the statement then it remains inadmissible. There is also nothing in theory preventing the documents being used in cross-examination (i.e. if they amount to a prior inconsistent statement), subject to the discretion of the court.[5]

Ultimately, the decision as to what is admissible in criminal proceedings will be a matter for the court. However, it is possible for the care judge, when granting disclosure of documents, to make a statement indicating that he or she considers the material inadmissible.[6]

7.2 AN EXCEPTION: VERBAL DISCLOSURES MADE BY PARENTS TO THE LOCAL AUTHORITY

The rules prevent the prosecution obtaining *documents* filed in the family proceedings.[7] There is, however, nothing to prevent the local authority sharing *oral admissions* received from a parent unless that information has subsequently been put into documents filed with the court.[8] The court's leave is, however, required before those other than social workers may disclose information to third parties (e.g. Children's Guardians and experts).[9]

---

[4] Swinton Thomas LJ, *Re EC (Disclosure of Material)* [1996] 2 FLR 725.
[5] *Re L (Care: Confidentiality)* [1999] 1 FLR 165.
[6] See, for example, Wall J, *Re AB (Care Proceedings: Disclosure of Medical Evidence to Police)* [2002] EWHC (Fam) 2198.
[7] See Chapter 3, section 3.3.
[8] *Re G (A Minor) (Social Worker: Disclosure)* [1996] 1 WLR 1407.
[9] *Re L (Police Investigation: Privilege)* [1997] AC 16; [1996] 1 FLR 731.

CHAPTER 8

Public interest immunity

8.1 OVERVIEW

Information held by a local authority (LA) in respect of any individual is confidential and subject to the Data Protection Act 1998. Information can only be disclosed to third parties in certain specified circumstances, and otherwise can only be disclosed with the consent of the data subject or by order of the court.

Frequently, LAs are requested, either by defence solicitors or by the Crown Prosecution Service (CPS), to disclose information from their social services files relating to investigations or information received in respect of children. On receipt of a request of this kind, the LA will consider carefully whether the requested material is to be disclosed voluntarily. Where it is not prepared to disclose material voluntarily, the LA will assert that the information is immune from disclosure on the basis that it is not in the public interest to disclose, hence the formulation of the phrase 'public interest immunity' (PII).

Over the last few years more and more requests for access to social services files have been received by LAs and there are a number of local area protocols which have been set up between the LA, police, local criminal solicitors and the Crown Court, in order to ensure consistency of practice and compliance with evolving case law (see Appendix 2).

An LA cannot simply hand over information on its files to the defendant in criminal proceedings, without considering first if the disclosure is legally appropriate. There is a statutory duty to preserve confidentiality under the Data Protection Act 1998 unless one of the exceptions in the Act applies, and there may be other legal constraints on the disclosure of information. The policy behind the public interest in confidentiality is, of course, to protect relationships with clients, to encourage those involved to be able to express opinions freely in confidential meetings, to protect sources of confidential information and to protect children. However, it may be right in a particular case to disclose the information voluntarily, without the need for a court order.

On many occasions the LA, having considered the case, will not be willing to disclose the material voluntarily. Where this happens, and the LA asserts PII, the court has the power to order disclosure of information held on the LA's files where it is satisfied that the balance of the public interest in fact lies in favour of disclosing the material. The applicable legislation in Crown Court cases is Criminal Procedure (Attendance of Witnesses) Act 1965, s.2. This Act enables the person who wants the material (often defence solicitors) to apply to the court for an order requiring the LA to disclose the material.

8.2 *R v. READING JUSTICES, EX P. BERKSHIRE COUNTY COUNCIL* [1996] 1 FLR 149

This case sets out the proposition that those seeking disclosure under this legislation must satisfy the court that documents are 'likely to be material evidence'. In making that judgement, the following principles apply:

1. To be material evidence, documents must not only be relevant to the issues arising in criminal proceedings but also be documents admissible in evidence.

2. Documents desired merely for the purpose of cross-examination are not admissible in evidence.

3. Those seeking production must satisfy the court that the documents are likely to be material, this to include a real possibility though not probability.

4. The procedure should not be used as a disguise to attempt discovery.

There is an onus upon those applying to the court for a witness summons clearly to identify specific documents which must be material evidence that is relevant to the proceedings and admissible.

Where it receives notice of an application, the LA, amongst other things, will want to take a view on the relevance and admissibility of the material, and to do so will require the following information:

- defendant's and witnesses' names;
- addresses and dates of birth;
- a brief synopsis of what is being investigated;
- specific details of any allegations;
- a copy of the charges that have been made as they affect the complainant;
- full contact details of the defence solicitor and details of any defence;
- what specific information is required;
- what information is believed to be relevant;
- a copy of the indictment or schedule of charges.

Part 28.5 of the Criminal Procedure Rules 2005, SI 2005/384, which entered into force on 2 April 2007, requires notice of the application to issue a witness summons to be given to the person against whom the summons is to be issued. This person/LA will then have the opportunity to make representations in relation to whether it is appropriate for the witness summons to be issued.

The wasted costs regime should be borne in mind by those against whom witness summonses are made which are subsequently directed to be of no effect by the court. Courts can be referred to the case of: *Re: a Solicitor (Wasted Costs Order)* [1996] 3 FCR 365. Additionally, Prosecution of Offences Act 1985, s.19A(3) defines wasted costs as any costs incurred by a party as a result of any improper, unreasonable or negligent act or omission on the part of any representative or any employee of any representative.

If relevant information is identified on the LA's files, it is a matter of local protocol and practice as to how this information is disclosed. In some areas copies of relevant documentation are disclosed by the LA to the court, CPS and defence solicitors. In other areas files are flagged, submissions made by the LA and a paginated bundle of documents prepared for distribution to each party.

The process in cases involving a witness summons can be summarised as follows:

(a) request for access to files, together with detailed information relating to allegations, materiality, relevance and admissibility;

(b) response from agency holding file;

(c)   application, on notice, for witness summons;

(d)   documents are identified by the agency holding information and response to witness summons;

(e)   documents flagged and disclosure considered by the judge;

(f)   where the judge orders disclosure, the agency holding information discloses relevant documentation.

CHAPTER 9

Special measures

9.1 OVERVIEW

The table below sets out the special measures provided in the Youth Justice and Criminal Evidence Act (YJCEA) 1999.

Special measure	Reference in YJCEA 1999	Section 16 witnesses (children and vulnerable adults)	Section 17 witnesses (intimidation/ fear or distress)
Screening witness from the accused	s.23	Full availability	Full availability
Evidence by live link	s.24	Full availability	Full availability
Evidence given in private	s.25	Full availability	Full availability
Removal of wigs and gowns	s.26	Full availability in Crown Court; not applicable in magistrates' court	Full availability in Crown Court; not applicable in magistrates' court
Video recorded evidence-in-chief	s.27	All children under 17 and vulnerable adults in Crown Court. Children in need of special protection only in magistrates' court and Youth Court	Video recorded evidence-in-chief will be available in England and Wales for complainants in all sexual offence cases tried in the Crown Court, where the investigation into the offence commenced on or after 1 September 2007

Special measure	Reference in YJCEA 1999	Section 16 witnesses (children and vulnerable adults)	Section 17 witnesses (intimidation/ fear or distress)
Examination through an intermediary	s.29	Partial availability – pilot areas only National roll-out announced in June 2007. Plans not yet fully prepared. No date set.	Not applicable
Aids to communication	s.30	Full availability	Not applicable
Live link for defendants under 18 and those 18 or over with a mental disorder or significant impairment of intelligence and social functioning	s.33A	Falls outside the special measures regime; available from 15 January 2007	Falls outside the special measures regime; available from 15 January 2007

9.2 CRIMINAL PROCEEDINGS

'Special measures' are available for vulnerable and intimidated witnesses in criminal proceedings under Part II of the YJCEA 1999.

'Vulnerable witnesses' are defined in YJCEA 1999, s.16 to include:

- all children aged under 17 years (in relation to all offences);
- adults who suffer from mental disorder; have a significant impairment of intelligence and social functioning; or have a physical disability or disorder (in relation to all offences).

'Intimidated witnesses' are defined in s.17 to include:

- those whose quality of evidence is likely to be diminished by reason of fear or distress in connection with testifying in the proceedings, taking into account the nature and alleged circumstances of the offence or their personal circumstances and any behaviour towards them of the accused or associated persons.

Special measures provide the court with a menu of options for the way a witness gives evidence, including:

- use of screens around the witness box in the courtroom;
- video recorded evidence-in-chief;
- use of live link for cross-examination and re-examination;
- giving evidence in private (in certain cases);
- intermediaries and communication aids (for vulnerable witnesses in certain parts of the country);
- removing the use of wigs and gowns in court.

Special measures should be discussed between the witness and the police officer taking their statement. The measures are available across the country with the exception of video recorded evidence-in-chief and intermediaries, which are subject to phased implementation. Details of the current availability of these two measures can be found in Ministry of Justice Circular dated 25 June 2007.[1] Enquiries about the availability of these two measures should be made to the relevant regional CPS office or the Office for Criminal Justice Reform.

All child witnesses in cases involving sexual or violent offences (deemed 'in need of special protection' by virtue of YJCEA 1999, s.21) may give pre-recorded examination-in-chief in the Crown Court and the magistrates' court and Youth Court, subject to an interests of justice test. In other cases, child witnesses may give pre-recorded examination-in-chief in the Crown Court only, again subject to the interests of justice test.

Other vulnerable or intimidated witnesses (including all victims in sexual offences cases) are eligible for special measures provided that they fall within the criteria in s.16 or s.17 and the measure applied for will maximise the quality of their evidence.

Live link evidence is the norm for children subject to the requirements of the 'Primary Rule' in YJCEA 1999, s.21, and with effect from 15 January 2007 is available for defendants under 18, or those 18 or over with a mental disorder or significant impairment of intelligence and social functioning (see YJCEA 1999, s.33A). Giving evidence by live link is mandatory for a child in need of special protection (see YJCEA

---

[1] Available via the Law Society or Criminal Bar Association websites: **www.lawsociety. org.uk** and **www.criminalbar.com**.

1999, s.21(1)(b)(i) and (3)(b) and s.24). A child not in need of special protection must give evidence by live link unless it would not maximise the quality of the witness' evidence (YJCEA 1999, s.21(4)(c)).

If a witness has any concerns about safety, these should be discussed with the police and/or the Witness Care Unit.

9.3 FAMILY PROCEEDINGS

There are no specific legislative provisions relating to special measures in family proceedings. Most family cases are heard in private and therefore closed to anyone not a party to, or appearing in, the proceedings. The child's wishes and feelings are reported to the court through the officer appointed as Children's Guardian (in care proceedings) or Cafcass reporter (in private law proceedings). The judge may, if appropriate, ask to meet with the child in the judge's chambers to explore the child's wishes, if the child is willing to do so, and such discussions will be reported back to the parties. Children generally do not give formal evidence in family proceedings.

Many family courts have special facilities for vulnerable parties – separate exits, entrances and waiting areas might be available to ensure parties are safe while they attend. All care centre courts also have access to remote video link facilities.

In any proceedings involving safety concerns, contact should be made with the court's Accommodation Officer or Security Officer, who will be able to advise whether appropriate arrangements are in place. If special facilities cannot be provided then a request can be made to transfer the case to a court able to provide the facilities needed.

CHAPTER 10

Common difficulties, practical examples and frequently asked questions

10.1 COMMON DIFFICULTIES

Difference of approach between the family and criminal jurisdictions

Problems can arise because of a fundamental difference of approach between the family and criminal jurisdictions. The police/Crown Prosecution Service (CPS) frequently want to keep the developments in their investigation confidential at least until after they have interviewed the parents about them. This can take a considerable period of time, especially if they are waiting for the results of forensic examinations. It is entirely understandable from the point of view of the criminal investigation that the police wish to be able to use their evidence so as to have the best chance of eliciting an admission from the accused – i.e. with the element of surprise. In family proceedings, on the other hand, the court and parties will want to press ahead with the preparation of their case for the fact-finding hearing which is expected to take place as soon as possible. They will find the wait for the next bail date – and the next round of police interviews – frustrating, and it is likely to cause a delay in the preparation of the civil trial.

Delay

There can be a tendency, especially where the evidence is not straight-forward, for each investigating authority to be waiting on the results of the investigation of the other. The local authority (LA) is awaiting the outcome of police interviews while the police may be awaiting the outcome of the civil investigation – or even the actual findings of the judge. There is a risk that each investigator loses an element of momentum in the hope that progress will be made by the other. Again, closer liaison between the authorities should reduce the risk of unrealistic expectations and unnecessary delay.

Personnel

It is crucially important to identify as early as possible a sufficiently senior person in each investigation with authority to keep his or her counterpart informed of progress on a consistent and ideally agreed basis. When this step is not taken, there can be a muddled or incomplete exchange of information. During care proceedings, the solicitor representing the LA may be the best person with whom to keep in touch.

Chinese walls

The practice is now well established that an adult defendant will be represented by separate criminal and civil legal teams. Liaison between the two teams is surprisingly often very limited owing to practitioners being unduly guarded about volunteering any information that might jeopardise their case. There is often no reason for the one team to keep the other in the dark – at least not to the extent that happens on a routine basis. If the two teams liaise efficiently, resources could be saved seeking disclosure, for example where the defendant's criminal team already has documents which can be filed in the civil proceedings (subject to the necessary permission being sought from the CPS).

Status of criminal statements in civil proceedings

Once police evidence is filed in civil proceedings it is likely, in a complex case, to be quite voluminous. Many witnesses are interviewed by the police even if they are relatively peripheral to the investigation. On a practical note, the parties in the civil proceedings often fail to give proper consideration to the status of that evidence. It is rare that the LA will wish – or need – to call many of the witnesses, and yet it may wish to refer to matters contained in those witness' statements. There are various ways to deal with this issue: there can be an order that the statements do stand as evidence in the civil proceedings; there can be an agreement – or order – to the effect that the LA must identify and call the core witnesses on which it seeks to rely. What is important is that

72

this issue is considered and resolved in good time so that witnesses who are required to attend the civil trial are warned and available when necessary. It is good practice for the police to inform these witnesses of the potential for them to give evidence in both the civil and criminal cases.

Weight of criminal conviction in family courts

The verdict in a criminal court which comes first in time before a final family court hearing will be given great weight by the family court. In a civil (family) court, a conviction for an offence, once formally proved by the relevant documentation, establishes the commission of that offence unless the defendant proves that he or she did not commit the offence.[1] The burden of disproving the conviction would be on the defendant, and would be on a balance of probabilities. In practice, however, a conviction is usually decisive. The standard of proof is of course higher in the criminal court, and whilst the family court is not bound by findings in other proceedings, it would be an exceptional case in which the family court would deem it reasonable to re-open the issues tried before a criminal court.

Weight of family court findings in criminal courts

The findings made by a family court are not admissible in the criminal court. The standard of proof is of course lower than that applied in the criminal jurisdiction, and the criminal court is obliged to conduct its own fact-finding exercise. A finding of 'not proved' in a family court is not conclusive of criminal proceedings, and does not affect the Crown's discretion to prosecute.[2] The family court's findings may, however, be highly relevant to the CPS in its decisions relating to charge, and to the court's views on sentence.

---

[1] Civil Evidence Act 1968, s.11(2).
[2] *R* v *SL* [2006] 1 WLR 3092; [2007] 1 Cr App R 1; [2007] 1 FLR 462; [2007] Crim LR 472.

10.2 PRACTICAL EXAMPLES OF DIFFICULTIES CAUSED AT THE CRIMINAL/FAMILY INTERFACE

Example 1: Care proceedings already underway when suspicions about injuries to the child are raised

The child lives with his father and his father's partner. Following general concerns about the family, an interim care order is made and parenting assessments are underway, whilst the child remains in the home. Social services involvement has been considerable, but nevertheless the LA comes to the conclusion that the father is probably unable adequately to parent the child, and a permanent alternative placement is necessary. A child protection medical examination is arranged in November, and x-rays show many fractures to the child's limbs, of differing ages, which are felt to be non-accidental. The child is removed to foster care.

A timetable had already been put in place for a final care hearing in June/July. It is clearly necessary that a finding be made in relation to the injuries. The police indicate that they want to interview the father and his partner; in the meantime the police refuse to allow the LA to release copies of the medical records relating to the injuries to any of the parties or their lawyers involved in the care case, not even those acting for the child. The police will not release into the care proceedings any of the evidence they obtained by interview. Attending court to oppose disclosure orders in relation to the medical reports, the police officer indicates that they are not in a position to re-interview the father until February of the next year, and will not release information in their possession until after the interview has taken place. The delay incurred within the care proceedings is such that the final hearing date is lost and is re-listed for November. The care plan remains one of permanent placement outside the family, but the plan cannot be pursued in the absence of a causation hearing. The child will have been in short-term foster care for 12 months by the time the final care hearing takes place. The father is ultimately charged with neglect.

Example 2: Care proceedings alongside criminal investigation

A baby is brought injured to hospital and subsequently dies; the cause of death is unclear. Police and the children's services department of the LA are immediately involved. Both parents are suspects, and the other children are removed under emergency orders. Care proceedings begin straightaway. Police arrest and interview the parents before releasing them on bail. By the time of the fact-finding hearing in the care proceedings, the police are still yet to decide whether to charge either or both parents, in the absence of any admission or any relevant forensic evidence. The family court makes a number of findings. There is no lack of goodwill between the investigating authorities, and in the end the necessary exchange of information takes place. The police decide not to charge any person, because, it is believed, of the lack of admissible evidence and the medical uncertainties.

The main problems in the investigation of this case were:

- *Delay.* It took a long time for the police to disclose their evidence despite an order in place providing for it to be obtained. This was due mainly to:

  (a) the inherent complexity of the case and thus the weight of evidence gathered;

  (b) the police desire to keep certain developments confidential until they had interviewed the parents about them under caution; and

  (c) the fact that the LA did not really know what documents existed and thus precisely what to ask for (although under the ACPO Protocol, it is sufficient to state the incident and concerns, and to require the police to state what documents are available).

  If there had been an ongoing 'progress report' made available by the police detailing the progress of the investigation and the nature of the evidence gathered, then any necessary application could have been made or request made on an informed basis.

  Ultimately, there was probably no way of avoiding the police desire for certain information to be released only after interview. Only rarely, if justified in the circumstances of a particular case, would the care judge make an order that risked compromising the integrity of the criminal proceedings.

- *Parents' fear.* The parents' fear of prosecution lay, it appeared, behind their continued denial in the care proceedings of any knowledge of the injuries to their child. The closer the police/LA liaison, of course, the more this inevitable fear will be fed. There is no way around this common feature of these cases save the continued careful use of Children Act 1989, s.98(2) where appropriate.

Example 3: Criminal proceedings conclude, before care proceedings, with acquittal

A baby is brought to hospital with head injuries and dies. A joint investigation ensues. Care proceedings begin in respect of other children of the family. Before that matter is tried, one parent is tried for murder and acquitted. In a subsequent fact-finding hearing in the care proceedings, findings are made against that acquitted parent.

Because the criminal trial has concluded, there are no difficulties in obtaining evidence from the CPS, including transcripts of part of the oral evidence given during trial. A huge number of experts had given evidence in the criminal trial, each instructed solely by one party in the proceedings. The main problem in the civil case is in *limiting* the evidence actually relied on during the care proceedings, and in managing the fact that the experts who came again to give evidence had originally been instructed unilaterally, rather than jointly as they would usually have been in care proceedings.

The exercise requires a tight approach from the LA, close judicial control and a responsible approach from the legal representatives of the parents.

10.3 FREQUENTLY ASKED QUESTIONS

1. How do I serve Part IV injunctions on a person in custody?

Service can be effected upon persons held in custody either by the relevant police officer or by an officer at the prison.

Contact details for the relevant police officer can be ascertained by contacting the relevant police force and citing the crime reference number (if you have it), or by giving the details of the offender. A list of contact details for all police forces in the UK can be accessed online (**www.police.uk/forces.htm**).

Contact details for each prison in England and Wales can be found online (**www.hmprisonservice.gov.uk/prisoninformation/locateaprison/**).

2. How do I send confidential information to a prisoner detained in prison?

Rule 39 of the Prison Rules 1999, SI 1999/728 allows for the sending of private legal correspondence. The rule states:

(1) A prisoner may correspond with his legal adviser and any court and such correspondence may only be opened, read or stopped by the governor in accordance with the provisions of this rule.

(2) Correspondence to which this rule applies may be opened if the governor has reasonable cause to believe that it contains an illicit enclosure and any such enclosures shall be dealt with in accordance with the other provision of these Rules.

(3) Correspondence to which this rule applies may be opened, read and stopped if the governor has reasonable cause to believe its contents endanger prison security or the safety of others or are otherwise of a criminal nature.

(4) A prisoner shall be given the opportunity to be present when any correspondence to which this rule applies is opened and shall be informed if it or any enclosure is to be read or stopped.

(5) A prisoner shall on request be provided with any writing materials necessary for the purposes of paragraph (1).

(6) In this rule, 'court' includes the European Commission of Human Rights, the European Court of Human Rights and the European Court of Justice; and 'illicit enclosure' includes any article possession of which has not been authorised in accordance with the other provisions of these Rules and any correspondence to or from a person other than the prisoner concerned, his legal adviser or a court.

Letters should be addressed to the prisoner, including their prison number, prefaced clearly with the phrase: 'Solicitor's Letter – Rule 39 Applies'.

3. How do I go about booking a legal visit to a prisoner in prison?

Each prison will have an officer responsible for booking legal visits. A request is usually required in writing (e-mail is often acceptable). A written response will be sent confirming the visit date and time, and the name of the visiting lawyer. Legal visits are not included in the prisoner's quota of family and friends visits per month (for which visiting orders are required).

Contact details for each prison in England and Wales, with legal visit booking information, can be found online (**www.hmprisonservice.gov.uk/ prisoninformation/locateaprison/**).

4. I am a family solicitor acting for a victim of domestic violence. She is asking for assistance in coping with being a witness in the criminal proceedings. Who can help her?

The police/CPS Witness Care Unit should assist her in understanding the trial process, and special measures available. The Victim Support Unit will also provide support. The support offered can include information on timescales, court attendance arrangements, court familiarisation, bail conditions and likely penalties.

5. I have heard that some integrated courts can hear both the family and criminal aspects of domestic violence cases, is this true?

Over 2006/2007 Croydon Magistrates' Court is piloting an Integrated Domestic Violence Court (IDVC) based on the New York model of 'one family, one judge' in which domestic violence cases are dealt with by a single court with dual criminal and family jurisdiction. The process is intended to ensure that there is efficiency and transparency at an early stage in both sets of proceedings. The IDVC in Croydon took its first case in November 2006, and an evaluation of the IDVC pilot will be conducted by HM Courts Service at the conclusion of the first year of operation.

6. What are Specialist Domestic Violence Courts?

There are now many Specialist Domestic Violence Courts in different areas of the country, with plans to expand the numbers. These are magistrates' courts which operate a clustering system for criminal cases involving domestic violence. Support and advocacy services are made available to victims, including help at court, and advice on housing, benefits and safety.

Some local areas have established specialist 'one-stop shop' resources for victims of domestic violence. In the London Borough of Croydon, for example, a Family Justice Centre[3] has been established to provide, in one centralised location, resources including medical and legal services, police officers, probation officers, doctors, counsellors, advocates, social workers, housing providers, benefit advice, education providers, children's services and adult education groups.

7. Who can enter family and criminal courts during proceedings?

Family proceedings are usually held in private (with some exceptions including appeals and committals). Only the parties, their legal representatives and interpreters have the right to be present during these proceedings. Witnesses and experts are generally only called into court when it is time to give their evidence. However, if a party feels they need to be accompanied into court by a friend, relative or supporter, they may wish to ask for the permission of the judge. This is a matter for the discretion of the judge, who may well seek the views of the other parties in court.

Access to criminal proceedings by the public is not generally restricted, although the court has certain statutory powers to exclude people from court in some cases involving intimidation of witnesses, and also has a common law power to regulate the proceedings of the court and remove persons from the court if necessary. Children under 14 are not permitted entry, except with the permission of the court in exceptional circumstances.

8. My client was the victim of an assault by her husband. How can I find out what the bail conditions are and whether the charges are going to be dropped?

The Code of Practice for Victims of Crime governs the services to be provided to victims of crime in England and Wales, by a number of organisations including the CPS, courts and police. If a suspect is released on police bail to appear at a court, the police must notify the victim of this event, the date of the court hearing and any relevant bail conditions. If the suspect is granted bail by the court, where an application was made to remand the suspect in custody, the police must

---

[3] See Croydon Council's website (**www.croydon.gov.uk/community/dviolence/fjcentre**).

inform the victim of that fact and also of any conditions attached to the bail that relate to, or involve or affect the victim and what the victim can do if conditions are broken. If, following charge and after review, the CPS decides to alter substantially or drop any charge, the CPS will notify the victim. In some types of cases – for example fatalities, child abuse or sexual offences – the CPS will also offer a meeting to explain the prosecution decision.

APPENDIX 1

Solicitors' information sheets*

INFORMATION SHEET FOR USE BY FAMILY PRACTITIONERS

Key information on concurrent criminal proceedings	
Incident date	
Offender/s Name: Date of birth:	
Victim/s Name: Date of birth:	
Officer in case Name: Tel: Fax:	
Police station details	
URN number	

* These sheets can be accessed in the electronic version of this publication (see **www.family-justice-council.org.uk**).

Crime reference number	
CRIS number	
Local CPS office	
Allocated CPS lawyer Name: Tel: Fax:	
Police/CPS Witness Care Unit Tel: Fax:	
Criminal defence solicitors firm Ref: Tel: Fax:	
Description of charges laid	
Criminal court details	
Outcome of last hearing Date: Outcome:	
Next hearing date	
Further relevant information	

INFORMATION SHEET FOR USE BY CRIMINAL PRACTITIONERS

Key information on concurrent family proceedings	
Court proceedings number	
Court	
Applicant/s Name: Date of birth:	
Applicant's solicitors Firm: Ref: Tel: Fax:	
Respondent/s Name: Date of birth:	
Respondent's solicitors Firm: Ref: Tel: Fax:	
Nature of application **(residence/contact/Part IV etc)**	
Outcome of previous hearings Date: Outcome:	

Orders made already Dates: Details	
Copies of orders requested/obtained from family solicitors?	
Next hearing date	
Date of listed final hearing	
Further relevant information	

Protocols and forms

ACPO POLICE/FAMILY DISCLOSURE PROTOCOL: DISCLOSURE OF INFORMATION IN FAMILY PROCEEDINGS

OBJECTIVE

The objective of this Protocol, which has been agreed between the Chief of Police for the [   ] and the Designated Family Judge for [   ], is to set out the mechanisms for the appropriate disclosure of police information in family proceedings in courts in the [   ] Area to provide the court with early information to enable it to properly determine any necessary direction(s) which need to be made in relation to documents, records or other evidential material held by the police in relevant criminal proceedings or investigations which may inform the Family Court (and the parties) in the determination of any factual or welfare issue within family proceedings, and:

- To provide timely advance notice to the Chief Officer of the existence of the family proceedings and the nature and detail of the information sought from the police

- To enable the police through the Chief Officer to indicate in advance what documents, records or other evidential material (including both used and unused material) is or may be available to be disclosed to the family court and whether there is any objection to or difficulty in the immediate disclosure of the same

- To assist the court (and the parties) in the framing of standard directions directed to the Chief Officer which will act (if necessary) as the conduit to process and deal with all such directions for disclosure affecting any division/borough of the [   ] Force Area without any undue delay

- To encourage early disclosure of full and frank information between the police, the parties and the Court subject only to the avoidance of prejudice to the proper conduct of ongoing police enquiries at the time of the request

UNDERSTANDING ON CONFIDENTIALITY

Police Information will not be disclosed unless there are important considerations of public interest to depart from the general rule of confidentiality. The protection of children is one of the areas where exceptions may be made.

Information supplied by the police in pursuance to this protocol is subject to the following implicit undertakings on the part of the parties and their legal representatives unless otherwise specifically directed by the court:–

- Any material disclosed will only be used for the purposes of, and preparation for, the current proceedings unless the permission of the Court is obtained;

- It will only be disclosed to professionals in the proceedings (and the parties) unless the permission of the court is obtained;

- The material will otherwise be kept confidential and copying should be kept to the minimum necessary to avoid the proliferation of copies of sensitive material.

- Where there is a Best Evidence or other video recorded interview one copy will normally be made available on request as soon as police investigations allow **either** by providing one copy to the Local Authority (if a party to the proceedings) or via the solicitors acting for either party in private law proceedings. Copies of Video recorded interviews will not be provided to unrepresented parties. Copying of video evidence should be kept to a minimum and consideration should be given to the parties attending the appropriate police station or local authority premises in order to view the copy video evidence at a mutually convenient time. Where this is not possible and the evidence has to be further copied, the party(ies) will meet the police reasonable costs of copying unless alternative arrangements have been agreed between the police and the parties legal representatives for making copies;

- In relation to any Best Evidence or other interview, parties' representatives will sign and abide by the terms of the police Standard Form of Undertaking in order to prevent the unauthorised dissemination / copying / use of the evidence. See Annex A – Form of

Undertaking – this form can be suitably 'adapted' to cover other evidence if necessary. Note, where the party is able to say that it is or is not necessary for the purpose of the proceedings for the video to be copied or available for viewing, the party should state so;

- That the police will not transcribe or make arrangements to transcribe any video interviews or tape-recorded interviews unless this has already been done in connection with a criminal prosecution/investigation.

PROPORTIONALITY

All parties should use the protocol proportionately having regard to what is reasonable, directly relevant and necessary when seeking disclosure from any third party.

This protocol may be departed from in exceptional circumstances and does not apply to genuine emergency situations.

Action	Party	Timing
1. Written Requests for Disclosure		
It is incumbent on parties to give very early consideration to what material held by the police may be relevant to the care or family proceedings. Whenever possible an early request for documents should be made to police prior to any hearing or application being made to the court.	Party requesting disclosure	Prior to any proceedings
The request should be made in writing and state precisely what evidence and information is sought and why in accordance with the Standard Request Form at Annex B. The police will normally respond to that request within 5 working days in accordance with the Standard Reply Form at Annex C. The Request Form should be sent to the nominated police disclosure officer or police representative identified in the Schedule below as the person to whom any request is to be sent or upon whom any order is to be served for the relevant Police Force Area.		
In the event the police are unable or unwilling to disclose the evidence or information requested without a court order it will be incumbent on the requesting party to make the appropriate application to court in accordance with the following procedure.		

Action	Party	Timing
2. Preparation for Request for Disclosure		
2.1 Preliminary Enquiries of Police		
Not later than 10 working days before the relevant hearing the solicitors for any party who proposes to ask the Court for a direction requiring the Chief Officer of any Police Force to disclose within family proceedings any document, record or other evidential material or information shall send by way of written Standard Request Form (Annex B) to the nominated police disclosure officer or police representative identified in the Schedule below as the person to whom any request is to be sent or upon whom any order is to be served for the relevant Police Force Area. This may renew or reiterate an earlier request made under 1 above. The Request Form should set out the following information: • The names and dates of birth of the parties including any relevant children and where possible, brief details of the circumstances of the incident(s) in respect of which the request is made • Any relevant addresses • The date and place of the specific incident or incidents upon which information is sought • The crime reference number (if known) • The name and 'collar' number (if known) of the Officer(s) in the case(s) • The nature and relevance of the documents, records or other evidential material sought • The date of the hearing at which the formal direction is to be sought • A draft of the proposed direction including the date by which the documents, records or other evidential material is likely to be directed to be disclosed (to be prepared in accordance with the wording of the public law Standard Variable Directions appended at Annex D wherever possible) • The likely timetable of legal and social work steps	The party proposing direction for disclosure of police evidence	10 working days before relevant hearing

Action	Party	Timing
• Whether and if so what date has been fixed by the court for any final hearing or fact finding hearing and whether the officer in the case is likely to be required at that hearing to give evidence.		
2.2 Police Response Not later than 5 working days before the relevant hearing the solicitors for the party proposing the direction be made for disclosure of documents, records or other evidential material or information shall obtain by way of written reply on the Standard Reply Form (see Annex C) from the nominated police disclosure officer or police representative identified in the Schedule below as the person to whom any request is to be sent or upon whom any order is to be served for the relevant Police Force Area (or on his/her behalf) the following information: • A list of what documents, records or other evidential material or information which have been requested are available. • If the police are not willing to disclose the evidence sought, the reason(s) why and when it is anticipated that the information can be provided. • Whether the documents, records or other evidential material or information can be provided within the timescale proposed by the draft direction provided • If the documents, records or other evidential material or information cannot be provided within the timescale proposed by the draft direction, the reason why they can not be so provided and the timescale requested by the police for their disclosure • Whether the police require the direction in relation to disclosure to be amended as to its terms from the draft provided, and if so in what terms do the police propose that the direction should be framed	The party proposing direction for disclosure of police evidence	5 working days before relevant hearing

Action	Party	Timing
• Where it is indicated that a police officer may be required to give evidence at any hearing, when that police officer is available to give evidence, and the dates and/or times to avoid. • The police Standard Reply Form or other letter in reply will always be filed with the court in advance of the hearing by both the police and the requesting party. • The police and/or a representative of the CPS shall be permitted to attend the hearing at which any request for disclosure from the police is to be made to make oral representations on the issue of disclosure, with or without Counsel.		
3. Hearing		
At the hearing where the request is made for disclosure the court shall consider: • The necessity and relevance to the issues required to be determined by the court, of the information sought to be disclosed. • The wording of the proposed direction for disclosure, with reference to Standard Variable Directions wherever possible. • The timing of any direction for disclosure with specific reference to any written representations by the police under 2.2 above. All disclosure directions should allow sufficient time for compliance which should in normal circumstances be 14 days. • The making of a request to the Family Section Manager that the court order be expedited in its preparation in accordance with the process described in the Schedule hereto and served within 24 hours by the court upon the nominated police disclosure officer or police representative identified in the Schedule below as the person to whom any request is to be sent or upon whom any order is to be served for the relevant Police Force Area.		

Action	Party	Timing
• Any necessary direction to the party making the request for disclosure, as to notice and service of the court order in accordance with this Protocol.		
4. Post-Hearing Action		
4.1 The solicitor securing the direction in respect of disclosure shall forthwith comply with the process described in the Schedule hereto and thereafter ensure that within 24 hours of the hearing the nominated police disclosure officer or police representative identified in the Schedule below as the person to whom any request is to be sent or upon whom any order is to be served for the relevant Police Force Area is aware of the terms of the direction made for disclosure.	The party securing direction for disclosure	Within 24 hours of directions hearing
4.2 The solicitor securing the direction in respect of disclosure shall forthwith upon receipt of the court order (or in the Magistrates Court on drawing up the order for the Court) and in any event within 2 days of the hearing serve the court order upon the nominated police disclosure officer or police representative identified in the Schedule below as the person to whom any request is to be sent or upon whom any order is to be served for the relevant Force Area.	The party securing direction for disclosure	Within 2 days of directions hearing

---

SCHEDULE TO PROTOCOL FOR DISCLOSURE OF POLICE EVIDENCE
SERVICE OF REQUESTS & ORDERS

ACPO Protocol requests should be sent to the named Protocol contact person in each Police Force Area. The identity of that person, and the details of the way in which the Protocol has been implemented in each Police Force, can be obtained from the central Domestic Abuse Coordinator for each local Police Force area. Contact details for each Police Force are available online (**www.police.uk/forces.htm**).

Following the relevant directions hearing the solicitors securing the direction for disclosure shall forthwith either:

a)   Obtain immediately from the court clerk a sealed copy of the order in the terms approved; or

b)   Attend at the court office with the approved order in the terms agreed (or, if attendance at the court office is not immediately practical send a copy by Fax) and arrange with the Family Section Manager (or such other representative of the court service as the Family Section Manager shall nominate) for the order to be drawn up and sealed immediately;

c)   In any event the order shall be made available to the party securing it to enable compliance with Protocol steps 4.1 and 4.2.

The address for service of any order can be obtained after consultation with the local Police Force, contact details for these being available online (**www.police.uk/forces.htm**).

ADDITIONAL INFORMATION

Where the information or documents sought do not relate to child abuse investigations and material is held by another unit, the relevant contact person will pass the request form to the unit or units holding, or likely to hold, the information or documents requested and will supply the contact details of this unit to the requesting party. It is then for that unit and the requesting party to liaise co-operatively over disclosure of the material sought and all further correspondence or contact should pass between them.

Witness Summons if necessary

Any requesting party may, if necessary, use the witness summons procedure to seek disclosure of specific files or documents outside the remit of the local Domestic Abuse Unit. This is of particular relevance to historic allegations or investigations into serious crime (e.g. murder, neglect, drugs offences, firearms offences). In such cases the requesting party may look to either the local Domestic Abuse Officer or the central Domestic Abuse Coordinator to identify the appropriate police unit likely to have the material. It is then for the requesting party to liaise with that unit and only if necessary to obtain a witness summons directed to an officer of that unit to bring the relevant file to court where disclosure of it or any of its contents can be ruled upon by the judge. Parties should avoid witness summonsing the Chief Officer since they will have no personal knowledge of the documents sought.

Proportionality

It is to be understood by all parties that the protocol should be used proportionately and is designed to facilitate only requests for items of evidence which the requesting party cannot, or cannot easily, obtain for itself, which only the police have and which are of central and not peripheral importance to the issues and incidents under consideration by the Family Court.

The following annexures can be obtained in electronic format by accessing this guide online (**www.family-justice-council.org.uk**).

ANNEX A

VIDEO TAPED EVIDENCE OF A CHILD WITNESS

CONFIDENTIALITY UNDERTAKING

UPON { Solicitor }..undertaking

1. To pay the reasonable costs incurred by the police in providing copies of the tapes referred to in the order ('tapes')

2. Not to cause or permit any further copies to be made of the tapes

3. To keep the tapes in a locked, secure container when not in use or in transit

4. To use his/her best endeavours to ensure that the tapes are kept within the personal custody of a single adult when in transit and not to deliver the tape to the Post Office or any commercial carrier

5. To release the tapes only to:

   (1) Counsel instructed in the case

   (2) any expert authorised by the court to prepare a report for use by the court

   (3) any other person only with the leave of the court

6. To require any person to whom the tape is released to sign a form of undertaking in the same terms as this undertaking.

7. To use his/her best endeavours to obtain the return of the tapes to his/her personal possession within 28 days of its release to any person

8. To permit his/her client to view the tapes only at his/her professional premises and in his/her presence

9. To return the tapes to the police forthwith upon his/her ceasing to be instructed in this matter and in any event within 7 days of the final hearing of this matter

10. To keep a written record of the name of any person allowed access to the tapes and the date of such access

ANNEX B

STANDARD REQUEST FORM FOR DISCLOSURE OF POLICE INFORMATION

[This form should be completed in accordance with the agreed protocol]

Police information will not be disclosed unless there are important considerations of public interest to justify departure from the general rule of confidentiality. These considerations include the protection of vulnerable members of society. The information below is provided on the strict understanding that such information is only for the use of the courts. It will be treated as confidential and will not be used for any other purpose.

ADVANCE NOTICE OF REQUEST FOR INFORMATION

Person Requesting Information

....

Job Title

....

[e.g., solicitor / social worker / Local Authority Disclosure Officer / Cafcass Officer]

Contact Telephone Number

....

Date of Request

....

CASE PROCEEDING AT (if underway)

....

HIGH COURT / COUNTY / FAMILY PROCEEDINGS COURT (delete as appropriate)

CASE NO

....

The next hearing date in this case is listed for ....

Advance notice of family proceedings and any request for [to indicate availability of] information should be made as soon as possible and at least 10 working days in advance of the relevant directions hearing date

Information is Required by [DATE] ....

> **Information should be received no later than 5 working days in advance of the hearing date**

Purpose of the Information *(delete as appropriate):*

Enquiries connected with Care Proceedings / Other Family Proceedings / Prospective Family Proceedings (please specify)

Request for Disclosure of Material held by .... **Constabulary/FSU/CPU**

Information Requested about the following person(s):

NAME (ALLEGED PERPETRATOR (S)):	NAME OF OTHER PARTY/PARENT [if applicable]:	
DoB:	DoB:	
ADDRESS:	ADDRESS:	
NAME(S) OF RELEVANT CHILD(REN) / (ALLEGED VICTIM(S)):	DoB	RELATIONSHIP TO ALLEGED PERPETRATOR

BRIEF DETAILS (INCLUDING DATE AND PLACE) OF THE CIRCUMSTANCES OF THE INCIDENT(S) IN RESPECT OF WHICH FAMILY PROCEEDINGS ARE BEING TAKEN / CONTEMPLATED

CRIME REFERENCE NUMBER (IF KNOWN):	NAME & COLLAR NUMBER OF OFFICER(S) (IF KNOWN):

BRIEF DETAILS (INCLUDING DATE AND PLACE) OF THE SPECIFIC INCIDENT(S) UPON WHICH INFORMATION IS SOUGHT.

PLEASE SET OUT THE NATURE OF THE DOCUMENTS, RECORDS OR OTHER EVIDENTIAL MATERIAL REQUESTED AND ITS RELEVANCE TO THE CIVIL/FAMILY PROCEEDINGS NOTED ABOVE: (List documents with as much particularity as possible eg father's interview, mother's statement, sister's video interview, medical report of Dr Jones etc)

DOCUMENT   RELEVANCE
1.
2.
3. etc

AN INDICATION OF THE PROPOSED DIRECTIONS FOR DISCLOSURE LIKELY TO BE MADE (INCLUDING THE DATE BY WHICH ACTUAL DOCUMENTS WILL BE REQUIRED) (list directions or attach draft order for directions)

THE LIKELY TIMETABLE OF LEGAL AND SOCIAL WORK STEPS:	

WHETHER AND IF SO WHAT DATE HAS BEEN FIXED FOR ANY FINAL HEARING/ FINDING OF FACT HEARING AND WHETHER THE OFFICER(S) INVOLVED IS LIKELY TO BE REQUIRED TO GIVE EVIDENCE
NO DATE FIXED / DATE FIXED FOR ....
FINAL / FINDING OF FACT HEARING
OFFICER(S) NOT REQUIRED / REQUIRED TO GIVE EVIDENCE {*DELETE AS APPROPRIATE*}

Signature of Person Making Request ....

PRINT NAME ....

ON BEHALF OF (NAME OF PARTY/ORGANIZATION ETC) ....

STANDARD POLICE REPLY FORM

REQUEST RECEIVED [DATE] ....

Information Found From Records held at ....

CONSTABULARY / FSU / CPU

Court Case Number (if applicable) ....

No Information Found *(delete if not applicable)*

NAME (ALLEGED PERPETRATOR):	NAME OF OTHER PARTY/PARENT [if applicable]:	
DoB:	DoB:	
ADDRESS:	ADDRESS:	
NAME(S) OF RELEVANT CHILD(REN) / (ALLEGED VICTIM(S)):	DoB	RELATIONSHIP TO ALLEGED PERPETRATOR

CRIME REFERENCE NUMBER (IF KNOWN):	NAME AND COLLAR NUMBER OF OFFICER/S (IF KNOWN):

THE NATURE OF THE DOCUMENTS, RECORDS OR OTHER EVIDENTIAL MATERIAL REQUESTED WHICH IS AVAILABLE FOR DISCLOSURE NOW: –

(LIST DOCUMENTS etc)

POLICE DOCUMENTS REQUESTED WHICH <u>CANNOT</u> CURRENTLY BE DISCLOSED

DOCUMENT [delete as appropriate]	WHEN Disclosure Could Be Made	COMMENT / REASON FOR NOT DISCLOSING
STATEMENTS – list of prosecution statements		

INTERVIEWS – with suspect under **Police & Criminal Evidence Act 1984** (list & date) (where applicable)		
ABE Video Interviews (list & date) (where applicable)		
MEDICAL REPORTS (where applicable)		
MISCELLANEOUS / OTHER documents – eg **CRIS/CRIME** reports etc (where applicable)		

POLICE Contact / Officer completing form .... (signature)

Tel. No ....

Disclosure Approved By .... **POLICE** Supervisor (signature)

Print Name .... **Rank/Number** ....

UNIT ....

ANNEX D

Standard Variable Directions relating to Police Disclosure

	DD: Disclosure of Court Documents and by Other Agencies
DD1	*Criminal proceedings concluded against a party* The solicitors for the (*identify party*) shall file and serve by (time/date) copies of the (identify documents *e.g. indictments/witness statements/ any written basis of plea placed before the court/pre-sentence report(s) prepared by the National Probation Service/and other reports before the court/transcript of the judge's sentencing remarks*) in relation to the proceedings in the Crown Court (include Calendar Number) in respect of which he/she was sentenced on the (insert date) (together with any record of previous convictions).
DD2	*Criminal proceedings against a non party* The Chief Constable of (*identify police force*) is requested to disclose forthwith (*or state time limit*) to (*identify local authority*):- (a) Copies of witness statements/records of interview/charge sheet/ other relating to the prosecution of (*identify relevant person*) pursuant to the complaint made by the (*identify relevant person/ party*) arising out of the incident (*specify incident and date(s)*); and (b) Copies of records of all/any-recorded complaints of incidents of domestic violence between (*identify persons or parties concerned*).
DD3	*Liberty to apply* Liberty to apply on not less than 48 hours notice is given to the Chief Constable in the event of any objection being raised to disclosure of the information required by paragraph (*insert paragraph number*).
DD4	*Ongoing criminal investigation* The Chief Constable of (*identify police force*) is requested to disclose to the local authority by (time/date) all statements/ entries in pocket notebooks/ transcripts of interviews/ photographs/ and other material (specify) in the possession of the police relating to the investigation concerning the injuries sustained by (*identity of child*) with liberty to the Chief Constable to apply to vary this order on not less than 48 hours notice (*or specify*).
DD5	*Disclosure of court documents to the police* Permission is given to the local authority to disclose forthwith copies of the statements/reports of the (*Identify parties/persons*) to (*identify police force*).

DD6	*Service of order on the police* The local authority/children's solicitor/other shall serve a copy of this order on the Chief Constable of (*identify police force*) forthwith
DD7	*Service of disclosed police records – domestic violence* The local authority shall file and serve by (time/date) copies of documents and records relating to complaints to the police of incidents of domestic violence (*identify persons/parties*) upon receipt of the same from the Chief Constable
DD8	***Domestic violence incident records*** The Chief Constable of <*name force*> is requested to disclose to the <*Party*> by 4pm on <*Date*> all records, FWINs or other relevant information in the possession of the police relating to all attendances made in respect of complaints relating to incidents of domestic violence at the addresses occupied by <*Name persons*> namely <*Addresses*> between <*Date*> and <*Date*>. Permission is granted to the Chief Constable to apply to vary this order on application to <*Case Management Judge*> on not less than 48 hours notice.

A SAMPLE PROTOCOL BETWEEN THE CROWN PROSECUTION SERVICE, POLICE AND LOCAL AUTHORITIES IN THE EXCHANGE OF INFORMATION IN THE INVESTIGATION AND PROSECUTION OF CHILD ABUSE CASES

1. PARTIES

The parties to this protocol are the [*name of the Local Authority*], [*name of Police Force*] and the Crown Prosecution Service.

2. AIM

The aim of this protocol is to provide an agreed framework between the parties for the sharing and exchange of relevant information in child protection enquiries for the purposes of criminal prosecutions in [*specify Area*].

3. OBJECTIVES

The objectives of this protocol are:

- To provide guidance in obtaining and sharing information between the Parties in order to protect the welfare of children by investigating and prosecuting offenders through the criminal justice system;
- To provide guidance that enables the Parties to apply a consistent approach to information sharing locally; and
- To foster a greater understanding between the Parties of their respective roles within the criminal justice system.

4. INTRODUCTION

4.1 Good practice calls for effective co-operation between the parties; working in the best interests of the child; and careful exercise of professional judgment based on thorough assessment and analysis of relevant information. This protocol is addressed to those who work in the investigation and prosecution of offenders in relation to child abuse cases.

4.2 The Parties recognise the fundamental importance of inter-agency working in combating child abuse. The Parties are committed to share information and intelligence between them where this is necessary to protect children as set out in the document entitled *Working Together to Safeguard Children*.

4.3 This protocol recognises:

(a) Social Services and Education departments of Local Authorities will always seek to act in the best interests of the children with whom they are involved; and

(b) The Police and the Crown Prosecution Service are bound by a duty to protect the confidentiality of material held by Local Authorities (dealing with the appropriate Social Services or Education department) and will not disclose to third parties, except with the leave of the court, or with the consent of the Local Authority, any material obtained directly or indirectly as a result of having access to material held by Local Authorities.

5. THE LEGAL FRAMEWORK

The duties of the Parties are set out in Annex A. The legal framework at Annex A, sets out the legal obligations, on which this protocol is based, of the Parties in relation to exchanging and sharing of information.

6. PROCEDURE

6.1 As soon as the Police investigating a suspected crime believe material exists within the Social Services and Education files which may be relevant to the investigation, they will notify the Local Authority by means of a written notice.

6.2 The Police will appoint, as appropriate, a suitably trained disclosure officer who will carry out the examination of relevant material on Social Services and Education files held by the Local Authority and whose task it will be to liaise with the Local Authority.

6.3 The written notice used by the police disclosure officer will include: (see attached draft letter at Annex B)

- The identity and contact details of the police disclosure officer;
- The identity and contact details of the officer in the case;
- A summary of the case and the details of the offences being investigated;
- A statement of the relevant information which is sought from the records in order to pursue all reasonable lines of enquiry, and why that information is thought likely to be relevant to the investigation;
- A statement of how failure to disclose relevant information would prejudice or delay the investigation.

6.4 Upon receipt of a request from the Police under 6.3, the Local Authority will appoint a suitably trained disclosure officer from the legal department who will liaise with the Police disclosure officer throughout the enquiry. The Local Authority disclosure officer will identify and collate relevant material from the Social Services/Education files which it is necessary to disclose for the purposes of the police investigation, in the light of the information provided by the Police in 6.3 above.* The review by the police will usually take place on Local Authority premises but may be elsewhere by agreement between the disclosure officers.

---

* At this stage, the local authority will disclose to the police information that is relevant for the purposes of the police investigation. This does not mean that the local authority, by so doing, is agreeing that the information disclosed to the police should in due course be disclosed to the defence. Such disclosure will be decided either by agreement between the local authority and the CPS or in default of such an agreement, an order of the court made under the CPIA.

6.5 The Local Authority will ensure that documents filed in family court proceedings are not included in the files to be seen by the police and/or Crown Prosecution Service. Where there are documents filed in family court proceedings, the Local Authority will provide a list of that material without describing what it is, in order for the police, if appropriate, to apply to the Family Court for disclosure.

6.6 The Local Authority will not reveal to the police relevant medical reports or other medical information without the consent of the author of that material. Where there is such material, the Local Authority will seek consent from the author to reveal it to the police. Where consent is refused, the Local Authority will inform the police that the material exists. The police and the Crown Prosecution Service may seek consent from the author of the material and/or apply for a witness summons to obtain the material.

6.7 When the Local Authority voluntarily discloses material to the defence they will reveal it to the police and/or Crown Prosecution Service. In addition, when the defence request material from the Local Authority under the Data Protection Act 1998, the Local Authority will notify the police and/or Crown Prosecution Service of the fact of that request.

6.8 The Police disclosure officer will be given priority to review the material following the agreed [see above] working day period. If there are difficulties in complying with the agreed timescale or if the material is ready for review more quickly, the Local Authority disclosure officer will notify the Police disclosure officer immediately.

6.9 Where the Police review the material, the Local Authority will accept that the Police may take notes or copies of the material as appropriate, as they require for the purposes of their investigation. The Police will accept that any material they read and any notes or copies they take are to be regarded as sensitive material which is subject to public interest immunity.

6.10 Any material identified by the Police disclosure officer during the review as being relevant to the issues in any criminal proceedings which may undermine the prosecution case or may reasonably assist any apparent defence case, must be brought to the attention of the Local Authority disclosure officer with a view to the Police disclosure officer obtaining a copy of the relevant documents. Any copy documents provided by the Local Authority to the Police will be treated as sensitive material which is subject to public interest immunity.

6.11 When the Police submit a full file to the Crown Prosecution Service, including all correspondence between the Police and the Local Authority, the Police disclosure officer will identify all unused material on the appropriate (MG) forms and in particular material that is viewed and obtained from the Local Authority. It will be the duty of the Police disclosure officer to identify any material which might undermine the prosecution case or might reasonably assist the defence case.

6.12 In the event of further relevant material coming into the possession of the Social Services and Education departments, the Local Authority disclosure officer will disclose to the Police disclosure officer that material and will provide a continuous opportunity to review and take copies of that material. Further, it is accepted by the Local Authority that as an enquiry develops, the material may have to be re-visited.

6.13   On receipt of the full file the Crown Prosecution Service will review the unused material in accordance with its statutory duties under the Criminal Procedure and Investigations Act (CPIA) 1996.

6.14   The Crown Prosecution Service shall treat all material disclosed by the local Authority as sensitive material.

6.15   Where any Local Authority material reviewed by the Crown Prosecution Service falls within the statutory disclosure tests under the CPIA, the Crown Prosecution Service shall write to the Local Authority disclosure officer, within [ ]* days of review, setting out the reasons why the material falls to be disclosed and informing them of that decision. Within [ ]* days of receipt of that notification, the Local Authority disclosure officer shall be given an opportunity to make any representations in writing to the Crown Prosecution Service on the issues of disclosure.

6.16   The Crown Prosecution Service will not disclose any material to the defence unless by agreement with the Local Authority or by order of the court following a public interest immunity application.

6.17   If the Local Authority agrees with the Crown Prosecution Service to disclose material identified by the Crown Prosecution Service which falls within the statutory disclosure tests under the CPIA, the Crown Prosecution Service will disclose the material to the defence.

6.18   If the Local Authority asserts public interest immunity and objects to disclosure, to the defence, of any material identified by the Crown Prosecution Service which falls within the statutory disclosure tests under the CPIA, the Crown Prosecution Service will make a public interest immunity application to the court as soon as reasonably practical. The Crown Prosecution Service will notify the Local Authority of the date and venue of the public interest immunity application and inform the Local Authority of their rights to make representations to the court under the Crown Court (Criminal Procedure and Investigations Act 1996) (Disclosure) Rules 1997 and the Magistrates' Court (Criminal Procedure and Investigations Act 1996) (Disclosure) Rules 1997.

6.19   Following receipt of a defence statement, the Police disclosure officer will send a copy of the defence statement to the Local Authority disclosure officer.

6.20   The Local Authority disclosure officer will reconsider the relevance of the material held by the Local Authority in the light of the defence statement. Where the Local Authority identify further material to be revealed, the Local Authority disclosure officer will notify the Police disclosure officer of that material.

6.21   The Police disclosure officer will review that material held by the Local Authority and any material previously revealed to the Police for the purposes of carrying out secondary disclosure. The Local Authority disclo-

---

* To be agreed between local signatories.

sure officer will arrange for the material to be available for further review by the Police disclosure officer within [ ]* working days of receiving a written request. The Local Authority disclosure officer will retain a copy of the defence statement.

6.22 In the event of the defence making an application under section 8 of the CPIA for further disclosure of material held by the Local Authority and already considered by the Police and/or the Crown Prosecution Service in the criminal proceedings, the Crown Prosecution Service will liaise with the Police and Local Authority disclosure officers prior to the hearing of the application.

6.23 Where the defence apply for a witness summons against the Local Authority for disclosure of material not in the possession of the Police or the Crown Prosecution Service, the Local Authority will inform the Police disclosure officer and the Crown Prosecution Service of the time and place of the hearing of the witness summons and the nature and grounds of such an application.

6.24 The Prosecutor has a duty to keep under continuing review the question of whether there is any unused material, which might undermine the prosecution case or might reasonably assist the defence case. The Parties recognise that they may need to review the material again if other issues become relevant during the course of the criminal proceedings.

6.25 In the event that there are no criminal proceedings, or the proceedings are discharged, or the accused is acquitted, the police and/or Crown Prosecution Service will return all material in their possession belonging to the Local Authority.

7. SCHOOLS AND OTHER ORGANISATIONS INVOLVED IN THE CARE OF CHILDREN

7.1 Where the Police investigating a suspected crime believe material exists with Schools the Police should contact the Local Authority to identify the status of the school. Where the Local Authority identifies the school as an Independent School, it should inform the police, so that the police may approach the school directly to obtain the material.

7.2 The Parties to this protocol would encourage other organisations that are involved in the care of children, to follow the provisions laid down in this protocol in the sharing of information with the Police and Crown Prosecution Service in criminal proceedings.

8. MISCELLANEOUS PROVISIONS

8.1 In some cases to which this protocol applies a child concerned may be (or have been) the subject of court proceedings in the family jurisdiction. Nothing in this protocol authorises the disclosure of any document filed with the court in such proceedings or any information relating to them. This applies whether the proceedings are concluded or still pending. If material is identified that falls into this category then leave must be

* To be agreed between local signatories.

obtained from the court in which the family proceedings are being (or were) conducted.

8.2 This draft protocol does not diminish the existing legal rights of the Parties. Specifically, it will not operate to restrict the right of any Party to claim public interest immunity in connection with any material which has come within the ambit of the police investigation.

8.3 All signatories to this protocol accept that the protocol is entered into in good faith and on that basis all signatories will use their best endeavours to comply with their terms and the spirit of the protocol.

8.4 Effect should be given to this protocol locally by a suitable service level agreement between the Parties, and any other organisation that the Parties think appropriate.

8.5 Any disagreement over the workings of this protocol or local arrangements will be referred to the agreed level of management for early and informal resolution, wherever possible.

8.6 The Parties will at an agreed interval, monitor the workings of this protocol and any local agreement with a view to improving the efficiency and the well being of local professional working arrangements.

ANNEX A   LEGAL FRAMEWORK

INTRODUCTION

1. Professionals can only work together effectively to protect children if there is an exchange of relevant information between them. This has been recognised by the courts. In *Re G (a minor)* [1996] 2 AER 65 Butler-Sloss LJ said:

    'The consequences of inter-agency co-operation is that there has to be a free exchange of information between social workers and police officers together engaged in an investigation ... The information obtained by social workers in the course of their duties is however confidential and covered by the umbrella of public interest immunity ... It can however be disclosed to fellow members of the child protection team engaged in the investigation of possible abuse of the child concerned'.

2. Any disclosure of personal information to others must always have regard to both common law and statute law. This framework sets out the legal position of the local authority, police and the Crown Prosecution Service in relation to exchanging and sharing of information.

THE COMMON LAW OF CONFIDENTIALITY

3. Personal information about children and families held by the agencies is subject to the legal duty of confidence, and should not normally be disclosed without the consent of the subject. The law permits the disclosure of confidential information where a countervailing public interest can be identified. Such a public interest might relate to the proper administration of justice and to the prevention of wrongdoing. The court in *R v Chief Constable of North Wales Police, ex parte Thorpe* [1996] QB 396 Lord Bingham CJ considered that where a public body acquires information relating to a member of the public which is not generally available and is potentially damaging, the body ought not to disclose such information save for the purpose of and to the extent necessary for performance of its public duty or enabling some other public body to perform its public duty.

4. There is a public interest in the prevention and detection of crime and in the apprehension or prosecution of offenders. Both domestic case law and the Data Protection Act 1998 recognise that it may be necessary for a local social services authority or education authority to disclose confidential material in its possession to the police for the purposes of a police investigation or criminal proceedings. The material to be disclosed must be both relevant and necessary for the purposes of the police investigation.

5. The information the Parties to this protocol possess will have usually come to the local authority from the individual him/herself and a range of other sources. There is no publication to any member of the public. The purpose of disclosure is to facilitate the more effective administration of justice, either by providing further evidence of criminal conduct or by revealing the hopelessness of cases that might otherwise have

reached the trial stage. Therefore, disclosure of material between the Parties to this protocol is permitted both by the general law on confidentiality and in particular by the law governing such disclosures by public bodies.

6. It is acknowledged that the law in the disclosure of confidential information is complex. There are restrictions on the sharing of information between the parties under the Data Protection Act and the Human Rights Act. However, the sharing of information is not necessarily contrary to these Acts.

DATA PROTECTION ACT 1998

7. The Data Protection Act 1998 (the 1998 Act) requires that personal information is obtained and processed fairly and lawfully; only disclosed in appropriate circumstances; is accurate, relevant and not held longer than necessary; and is kept securely. The Act allows for disclosure without the consent of the subject in certain conditions, including for the purposes of the prevention or detection of crime, or the apprehension or prosecution of offenders, and where failure to disclose would be likely to prejudice those objectives in a particular case.

8. When disclosing personal information, many of the data protection issues surrounding disclosure can be avoided if the consent of the individual has been sought and obtained. Where consent of the individual is not sought, or is sought but withheld, there can be an exchange of information between the Parties where there is an overriding public interest or justification for doing so. The Act contains general non-disclosure provisions, but sections 27–31 provide a number of specific exemptions. Section 29 covers crime. In the context of social services and education material, personal data processed for the purposes of prevention or detection of crime and the apprehension or prosecution of offenders is exempt from the first data principle (except to the extent to which it complies with the requirements of the second and third schedules of the 1998 Act).

9. Section 35 of the 1998 Act allows for disclosure by exempting data from the non-disclosure provisions (except to the extent to which it complies with the requirements of the second and third schedules of the 1998 Act), where disclosure is required by any enactment, rule of law, or an order of the court and, where disclosure is necessary for the purpose of, or in connection with, any legal proceedings (including prospective legal proceedings), or for the purpose of obtaining legal advice or is necessary for the purposes of establishing, exercising or defending legal rights.

10. This means that the exchange of relevant information between the Parties in this protocol is not restricted under the Act because it will nearly always be the case that the exemptions constitute an overriding public interest in favour of sharing the information.

CRIMINAL PROCEDURE AND INVESTIGATIONS ACT 1996

11. The Criminal Procedure and Investigations Act 1996 (the 1996 Act), the Code of Practice made under section 23 of the 1996 Act, and the

Attorney General's Guidelines on the disclosure of information in criminal proceedings, published November 2000, govern the disclosure of unused prosecution material to the defence. Guidance to the police and the Crown Prosecution Service is contained in the Joint Operational Instructions. The 1996 Act applies to all criminal investigations begun on or after 1 April 1997 and applies to a two-stage disclosure process. As soon as reasonably practicable after a not guilty plea in the Magistrates' Court, or service of the prosecution case, committal or transfer to the Crown Court, the prosecution must disclose to the defence any prosecution material that has not been previously disclosed and which might undermine the prosecution case (primary disclosure).

12. In Crown Court cases, the defence is required to provide, within 14 days of primary disclosure by the prosecution, a statement setting out in general terms their defence and particulars of any alibi witnesses. On receipt of the defence statement, the prosecution must as soon as reasonably practicable disclose any further material which may reasonably be expected to assist the accused's defence, as disclosed by the defence statement (secondary disclosure).

13. In Magistrates' Court cases, the defence may give a defence statement to the prosecutor. The requirements of a defence statement voluntarily given in Magistrates' Court cases are the same as those in Crown Court cases.

14. Throughout the proceedings, the prosecution is under a continuing duty to keep under review whether material should be disclosed to the defence. After the defence has provided a defence statement, the 1996 Act enables them to apply to the court for an order requiring the prosecution to disclose material if the defence considers that the prosecution has failed to comply with secondary disclosure.

15. Where the prosecution holds relevant sensitive material that meets the criteria for disclosure under the 1996 Act, then a public interest immunity application should be made to the court to withhold this material from the defence. Any decision to withhold such material is a matter for the court to determine.

16. Public interest immunity (PII) enables the courts to reconcile two conflicting public interests – the public interest in the fair administration of justice and the need to maintain the confidentiality of information the disclosure of which would be damaging to the public interest. PII is an exception to the general rule that all material which falls within the tests for disclosure must be disclosed. Special care needs to be taken in deciding where the balance lies between the two competing public interests.

17. The position of PII with respect to social services files has recently been summarised in *Re R (Care: Disclosure: Nature of Proceedings)* [2002] 1 FLR 755. Any person advancing a claim to PII in respect of material held by a local authority should set out with particularity the harm that it is alleged will be caused to the public interest. Before embarking on a claim for PII, consideration should be given to the question whether the

material passes the threshold test for disclosure under the Criminal Procedure and Investigations Act 1996, and if so why.

18. The Local Authority may assert PII but it is not necessary for them to do so in every case where disclosure is sought by the prosecuting authorities and for there to be a PII hearing before the court prior to disclosure taking place.

THE EUROPEAN CONVENTION ON HUMAN RIGHTS

19. The Human Rights Act 1998 gives effect to the rights and freedoms guaranteed under the European Convention on Human Rights. Article 6 ensures that every accused has the right to fair trial. It states that in the determination of his civil rights and obligations or of any criminal charge against him, everyone is entitled to a fair and public hearing within a reasonable time by an independent and impartial tribunal established by law. Article 8 protects the right to respect for private and family life, home and correspondence.

20. Article 6 is a 'special' right which means that it cannot be balanced against other public interests. On the other hand, Article 8 is a 'qualified' right which means that it can be interfered with where it is in the interests of national security, public safety or the economic well-being of the country, for the prevention of disorder or crime, for the protection of health or morals, or for the protection of the rights and freedoms of others.

21. The court will order disclosure of information regarding sexual and physical abuse of children (social service and education records) where it is necessary for an accused to have a fair trial (Article 6). The court will also order disclosure of the information where it is necessary for the protection of health or morals, for the protection of the rights and freedoms of others and for the prevention of disorder or crime (Article 8(2)). Disclosure should be appropriate for the purpose and only to the extent necessary to achieve that purpose.

JOINT INVESTIGATIONS

22. Section 26 of the 1996 Act provides that a person other than a police officer, who is charged with a duty of conducting an investigation with a view to it being ascertained, whether a person should be charged with an offence, or whether a person charged with an offence is guilty, shall have regard to any of the provisions in the Code of Practice made under the 1996 Act. Material obtained by social services in the course of an investigation under section 47 of the Children Act 1989, which may be obtained jointly with the police, but not in the possession of the police, is not subject to section 26. However, it is acknowledged that where such material is obtained jointly with the police, the local authority should as a matter of good practice, have regard to the Code of Practice.

23. Relevant material acquired during the course of a joint investigation should be given to the police disclosure officer and listed on a sensitive or non-sensitive MG form. If there is any disagreement between the police and the local authority on the material, then this will be resolved by the

Court by way of a public interest immunity application (see section 16 of the 1996 Act). Where material which has been jointly obtained is in the possession of the police, then that material is subject to the provisions of the Criminal Procedure and Investigations Act 1996.

24. In most cases social workers will be involved where the police are investigating allegations of sexual or physical abuse of children. In addition to complying with the 1996 Act, they should also adopt the Attorney General's guidelines and have regard to Article 6 of the European Convention on Human Rights.

NON-JOINT INVESTIGATIONS

25. Where a person subject to a criminal investigation has not been charged, it is often the case that the investigating police officer will require to know about the background of the complainant, family and associates. Such information may be helpful in assessing the veracity of any complaint and the likelihood of conviction. Occasionally, if the local authority had disclosed material to the police at an earlier stage the person under investigation would not have been charged.

26. In these circumstances, the only mechanism to enable the investigators to make application to the court for the disclosure of such material is to consider whether it is appropriate to make an application for Special Procedure Material, under Schedule 1 of the Police and Criminal Evidence Act 1984. However, this is not a satisfactory approach because it goes against the ethos and spirit of the Parties exchanging and sharing information where it is necessary to protect children.

27. Therefore, where full details of the nature of the investigation and the reasons for requiring such material are given to the local authority and that the material is treated as confidential, then it is in the interests of justice for there to be disclosure of relevant material before charge. This would be considered 'necessary' in accordance with Schedule 3 of the 1998 Act.

28. Where a person has been charged with an offence and the social services and/or education departments of a local authority have not been involved in the investigation, but holds or is believed to hold material that could be relevant, then the local authority fall within the category of a third party. The procedure for the police in obtaining such information should be in accordance with this protocol.

29. Schedule 2 of the 1998 Act allows disclosure of non-sensitive material. Such material should be listed on a non-sensitive material form which will be sent, together with the material, to the police disclosure officer who will forward it to the Crown Prosecution Service.

30. The majority of the material held by a local authority will be of a confidential nature. Where the conditions are met in Schedule 3 of the 1998 Act, material should be revealed to the police disclosure officer and the Crown Prosecution Service. The material should be listed on a sensitive material schedule and this together with the documents should be given to the police disclosure officer and the Crown Prosecution Service. Where the local authority assert public interest immunity then section 16 of the

1996 Act provides that the court must not make a disclosure order unless a person claiming an interest in the material is given the opportunity to be heard.

31. Paragraphs 30–33 of the Attorney General's Guidelines refer to material held by other agencies, which includes a local authority. If it is believed by the investigator, the police disclosure officer or the prosecutor that it is reasonable to seek production of material held by the local authority and the request is refused then application should be made for a witness summons requiring production of the material to the court. The prosecution should be pro-active in such circumstances.

CONCLUSION

32. The aim of the protocol is to provide an agreed framework between the Parties for the sharing and exchange of relevant material in child protection investigations. While there is a difficult balance between the local authority complying with their duty of confidentiality, and the police and the Crown Prosecution Service obtaining relevant material from the local authority at the earliest stage possible in any criminal investigation, there are no legal reasons why the Parties should not exchange the material expeditiously, as outlined in this protocol. This would benefit everyone involved in any criminal child protection investigation and promote the efficiency of the criminal justice system.

Family-Criminal Interface Committee terms of reference

Composition

The Family-Criminal Interface Steering Committee was established on 9 February 2004, by the then Solicitor-General (Harriet Harman) and the former President of the Family Division (Dame Elizabeth Butler-Sloss, DBE) with the support of the Deputy Chief Justice. The Committee will be co-chaired by the Solicitor-General and the President of the Family Division. Management of the Committee has been delegated to its Deputy Chair, the Hon Mr Justice Hedley. The membership of the Committee will be representative of the key stakeholders involved in the interface between family and criminal proceedings. The Committee will be supported by a Secretariat based in the HM Courts Service and will consult with, and be supported by, all other relevant departments including the Department for Children, Schools and Families, the Home Office and the Department of Health.

Representatives from the magistrates' courts, police, Crown Prosecution Service, probation, Cafcass and social services will be invited to join the Committee in addition to the nominated representatives from the departments. The Committee will have the flexibility to co-opt additional members and may, from time to time, establish Working Parties to address specified tasks.

Terms of reference

The Family-Criminal Interface Steering Committee has been established to take an 'overview' role in coordinating all work currently being undertaken in England and Wales to improve the interface between the family and criminal jurisdictions. The Committee will identify issues that have not yet been addressed to meet the need to enable all stakeholders to respond more effectively to child protection, domestic violence and private and public family law issues within the forensic arena.

The primary objectives of the Steering Committee are:

1. to assess the effectiveness of the existing legal framework, structures and procedures, including primary and secondary legislation;

2.   to identify legislative, structural, procedural and other changes that may be required to improve the interface between the family and criminal jurisdictions;

3.   to recommend and prioritise changes identified to be acted on by government and the relevant stakeholders; and

4.   to identify and promulgate good practice on a consistent national basis for relevant stakeholders.

The Steering Committee is currently focused on:

1.   information sharing and exchange;

2.   joint directions hearings in concurrent criminal and family proceedings; and

3.   practitioner training.

APPENDIX 4

Useful contacts

The justice system

ACPO	www.acpo.police.uk
Cafcass	www.cafcass.gov.uk
Cafcass (Wales)	www.cafcass.gov.uk/cafcassCymru.htm
Court Service	www.hmcourts-service.gov.uk
Crown Prosecution Service	www.cps.gov.uk
Family Justice Council	www.family-justice-council.org.uk
Local Criminal Justice Committees	www.lcjb.cjsonline.gov.uk
UK Police Service	www.police.uk/forces/forces.htm

Government

Department for Children, Schools and Families	www.dcsf.gov.uk
Department of Justice	www.justice.gov.uk
HM Prison Service	www.hmprisonservice.gov.uk
Home Office	www.homeoffice.gov.uk
Legal Services Commission	www.legalservices.gov.uk

Further reading

Court Rules

Criminal Procedure Rules 2005

> **www.justice.gov.uk/criminal/procrules_fin/index.htm**

CPS materials

CPS (2001) 'Provision of Therapy for Child Witnesses Prior to a Criminal Trial (Practice Guidance)' (to be revised 2007)

CPS (2002) 'Provision of Therapy for Vulnerable or Intimidated Adult Witnesses Prior to a Criminal Trial (Practice Guidance)'

CPS (2006) 'Children and Young People – CPS policy on prosecuting criminal cases involving children and young people as victims and witnesses'

> These documents can be found at **www.cps.gov.uk** and **www.homeoffice.gov.uk**

CPS (2005) Code of Practice for Victims of Crime

> **www.cps.gov.uk/victims_witnesses/victims_code.pdf**

The Prosecutors' Pledge

> **www.cps.gov.uk/publications/docs/prosecutors_pledge.pdf**

Index